Job Success for Persons with Developmental Disabilities

DAVID B. WIEGAN

FOREWORD BY RON RUSH

Jessica Kingsley Publishers
London and Philadelphia

First published in 2009
by Jessica Kingsley Publishers
116 Pentonville Road
London N1 9JB, UK
and
400 Market Street, Suite 400
Philadelphia, PA 19106, USA

www.jkp.com

Library of Congress Cataloging in Publication Data
Wiegan, David B.
Job success for persons with developmental disabilities / David B. Wiegan ; foreword by Ron
Rush.
p. cm.
Includes bibliographical references and index.
ISBN 978-1-84310-922-8 (pb : alk. paper) 1. People with disabilities--Employment. I. Title.
HD7255.W537 2009
658.30087'5--dc22

2009007494

British Library Cataloguing in Publication Data
A CIP catalogue record for this book is available from the British Library

ISBN 978 1 84310 922 8

Printed and bound in Great Britain by
Athenaeum Press, Gateshead, Tyne and Wear

This book is dedicated to the hundreds of persons with developmental disabilities I have worked with over the last 31 years. I admire and respect their honesty, their hard work, their will to overcome challenges most of us would find overwhelming, and their seemingly infinite capacity to brighten a day. We can learn from them.

Contents

*F*oreword

Job Success for Persons with Developmental Disabilities illustrates a reality-based and commonsense approach to developing and maintaining employment opportunities for our most vulnerable (yet capable) population. The author discusses the value of meaningful employment for both the person with a developmental disability and society as a whole. He also pushes aside long-held beliefs about persons with disabilities and job development. Instead, he focuses on a business model that "employs positive, principle-based methods used to achieve win–win results for people with developmental disabilities and for the businesses employing them, in contrast to the ivory tower idealism often espoused by academicians."

The author shows the compatibility between the goals of business and those of the organization preparing the individual for employment in a business. David Wiegan has worked in the field of developmental disabilities for over 31 years. His philosophy for job development, placement, and maintenance is based on that experience.

Ron Rush, Executive Director
Marie Mills Center
Tillamook, Oregon

1

The Philosophy of Employment

Ask someone who they are, and their first response will very likely be the name of the job they do. Our employment defines us in a way that virtually nothing else could ever accomplish in a few words. We say we are a doctor, an accountant, a teacher, a cashier, a farmer, a writer, or some other job title. Each one of these titles (and thousands of others) communicates more about us in less time than anything else we might say. In a word or two we suggest our socioeconomic status, education level, and overall role in our society. These descriptors tend to be viewed with even greater significance than status regarding family, race, religion, or national origin.

It should be no surprise that people with disabilities have the same perfectly normal human perspective. They want to be viewed in the same light in terms of their contribution to their society. They want to be seen as individuals who have a legitimate role relative to the abilities they possess. The last thing they want is to be seen as merely "disabled," "handicapped," or whatever other deficiency-oriented view is used. *This seemingly simple concept is the fundamental principle in the philosophy of successful employment for persons with disabilities.*

The problem so many individuals with disabilities confront is that society in general often sees them in exactly the opposite way to how they want to be seen. They are typically labeled with a word or two, similar to the rest of us, but the description tends to be more of a diagnosis or statement of a condition they might have. Examples of this would be "retarded," "blind," "deaf," "epileptic," "paraplegic," and so on. Words are powerful, and they convey the thoughts and beliefs of the speaker. Therefore, when a word describing a perceived deficiency is used to define a person, the net effect can be very harmful to that individual's self-esteem. It is fundamentally de-humanizing. Even when it is done unintentionally, this tendency can create many serious problems. The irony, of course, is that the person already has more than enough challenges to overcome. The burdens that we, as the non-disabled, place on them in this manner may very often exceed those they were given by birth or circumstance. This is why successful employment is such an incredibly powerful instrument of positive change.

Success in a job valued by society can literally redefine a person. It can cause other people to forget about the disability and, instead, focus on the person and who he or she happens to be. Job success can instill confidence, energize the person, and enable self-esteem in a way that nothing else can approach. It can empower a person financially and provide opportunities to choose a course in life, in contrast to being told what to do. Most importantly, it allows a person to be regarded first and foremost as a person with *value* rather than a *diagnosis*.

Consider, for example, the disparity in perception we could expect in being introduced to someone using a wheelchair in two different scenarios. In the first, the person is in front of us having difficulty negotiating a malfunctioning door in the entry of a hospital. In the second, this same person is introduced to us as the physician who will be treating whatever problem brought us there. The status connoted by "physician" almost immediately normalizes the nature of the ensuing interaction, and the disability involved virtually disappears from the social equation. Regardless of what else we might otherwise ascribe to him or her, almost nothing would have such an immediate, profound, and overall positive effect on our perception.

Our focus in this book will be on people with developmental disabilities, a group of disabilities typically involving intellectual impairments. Usually included in the definition are mental retardation, cerebral palsy, severe epilepsy, autism spectrum disorders, and others posing similar kinds of challenges. The definition is broad enough to include some individuals with normal intellectual capacities, but they are the exception to the rule. Because the definition implies that some assistance is needed on a sustained and lifelong basis, people with developmental disabilities very often have some of the greatest challenges to overcome in becoming successfully employed. Nevertheless, success is possible and just as essential as it is for anyone else. Unfortunately, many (if not most) people with developmental disabilities remain unemployed, underemployed, or employed in jobs poorly matched to their talents. Many governmental agencies, non-profit organizations, businesses, and private contractors engage in the pursuit of employment for them, and spend many millions of dollars in the attempt. The progress that has been made in the last few decades has been nothing short of miraculous, but we still have a very long way to go. There are many reasons for this, and some are quite unexpected. Many of the problems in the systems and organizations involved reside in the underlying philosophical premises they embrace. We shall identify them, and also promote principles and techniques that have proved to be effective.

Job success for persons with developmental disabilities is more than a benefit to the individuals themselves. While it is true that there are certainly costs associated with providing the necessary assistance, it is also true that the economic benefits to society far outweigh these costs. Each person employed successfully ultimately requires less and less assistance in other forms such as welfare, food stamps, social services, and so on. There is an old saying along the lines of "the best social program is a good job," and it is profoundly true. Good employment is an inherently beautiful problem-prevention technique, and prevention of problems is far less expensive than attempting to deal with them after the fact. People who are gainfully and satisfactorily employed tend to invest in maintaining their jobs. As a result, they are far less likely to engage in self-destructive practices involving drugs, theft, or other criminal activity. Furthermore, persons with developmental disabilities who are employed become taxpayers and contribute to society economically as well. The proverbial bottom line is that employment simply makes good sense from an economic perspective as well as from a philosophical perspective. Furthermore, it is simply the right thing to do.

Service programs for persons with developmental disabilities have evolved a great deal over the years. As recently as the 1950s many of these people were still hidden from public view or committed through courts to a life sentence in an institution. This was a form of segregation as despicable as any, and it was practiced with the blessings of professionals in medicine and psychology. Some went even further than segregation. Adolf Hitler's attempts to eradicate segments of the population targeted people with disabilities as well as Jews and others. This fact alone should be prima facie evidence as to the inherent malevolence of segregation and discrimination. All citizens, being created equal (even if some have disabilities), have inalienable rights to life, liberty, and the pursuit of happiness. These rights are taken away if the people in question are segregated from their own communities. It is that simple.

Advocacy organizations began to make substantial impacts during the 1960s, and a de-institutionalization campaign continued for several decades. Community-based service organizations were developed and gradually replaced most of these institutions in the United States. The concept of "supported employment" became a real option in the late 1970s and 1980s. *Supported employment* means that a person with a disability works in a job in a community setting but continues to receive support services. The term is widely used but often misunderstood, even by professionals in the field. It is not, for example, synonymous with "competitive employment," a term used to describe normal employment which does not require any special support services. Because, by definition, persons with developmental disabilities typically require some kind of ongo-ing support services, competitive employment is seldom a realistic option. Having said that, supported employment over a period of time, and embracing other kinds of support (such as that voluntarily provided by employers), can approach competitive employment in terms of wages, independence, and other measures of success. The huge problem still unresolved is that so many persons with devel-opmental disabilities have not achieved real success. The reasons are varied but often have a root cause embedded in the academic training of the professionals involved.

Many practitioners in the developmental disabilities service field come from social service backgrounds. These are often termed the "helping professions," and they certainly have a legitimate role. When it comes to employment success, however, many of these professionals are poorly prepared to be of much help at all. The reason for this is that social services' academic training tends to focus on providing services to people who need their services, and (somewhat ironically) they themselves need to be needed in return. This creates a kind of symbiotic relationship which is detrimental to furthering the cause of independence for their clients. Further, it tends to assume that government-funded services are the solution to problems, and that private businesses are the enemies. These kinds of philosophical premises are not overtly stated, but are reflected by the actions and statements of those who end up as professionals in the field.

This book is dedicated to successful employment based on a business model. It employs positive, principle-based methods used to achieve win–win (with apologies for the cliché) results for people with developmental disabilities and for the businesses employing them. In contrast to the ivory tower idealism often espoused by academicians, every single technique herein is based on over 30 years of real life time-tested professional experience, and makes sense economically for everyone involved. It will show in great detail exactly how to develop and sustain life-changing employment success for those who need it the most. It will take the reader into the minds of business managers, and help us to understand what they have to consider when hiring persons with disabilities. Most importantly, it will show the profound impact on the quality of life a good job can achieve. There is surely no greater outcome imaginable in any helping profession.

2

*T*he Business Model

In order to understand the business model as it relates to the purpose of this book, we need to understand business from the perspective of owners and managers. Businesses exist to create a profit for those who risked their capital in the creation of the business. Profit is their primary mission, and it is an inherently positive and normal expectation for any business. Any organization should have a clear mission identifying its purpose of existence, and profit *per se* is as legitimate as any other. Non-profit organizations have a different kind of mission, and this is as it should be. The very idea of profit sometimes creates animosity when destructive means are employed to reach this end, but the end itself is not the problem. Rather, it is the inappropriate means utilized in its pursuit. Likewise, non-profit businesses also sometimes employ inappropriate means in the pursuit of goals outside of their stated mission. In either case, legitimate ends do not justify illegitimate means.

If businesses and their profits did not exist, there would be no government-funded service programs because there would be no money for them. All social services are funded indirectly by business profits, in the form of business or individual taxes or donations otherwise not possible without profits at some point. If there were no profits there would be no services to the people who need them. The role of the government as fashioned by our founding fathers was to safeguard our individual rights, and it should create and enforce laws to accomplish this goal. We all know that some businesses (like some individuals) exploit for personal gain at the expense of others. This is not legitimate capitalism—it is simply theft, cronyism, or manipulation. Legitimate businesses create wealth by adding value to the products and services they provide to willing customers. We shall not concern ourselves with those businesses which masquerade as legitimate but derive their earnings solely at the expense of others, or are forced on unwilling customers through inept legislation. There are plenty of them, of course, and their numbers exist in direct proportion to the failures of government to create and enforce laws limiting these exploitations.

The vast majority of businesses are run by honest, hard-working people trying to make a good living. The best employers and their employees share the goal of mutual sustained prosperity. The law of the jungle in business is that revenues must exceed expenses or the business ultimately ceases to exist. The excess of revenues over expenses is profit, and the amount of profit must exceed the amount that less-risky investments would earn or the investment would not have been made and the business would not exist. This is simple Economics 101, like an introductory class in a US college. Yet, as simple as this is, many social service professionals seem to labor under the illusion that there is a vast imaginary storehouse of money somewhere, and that nasty business managers just refuse to share it with them. The wealth-sharing belief is, essentially, a premise of socialism and it does rear its head (albeit covertly) in social services far more often than we would like to believe. This fact must be pointed out and acknowledged because otherwise the many failures associated with job placement programs are doomed to be repeated. *Successful job placements require understanding and acceptance of the realities of business.* This point is emphasized here because it is critically important to successful job placements. Social work colleges would do well to incorporate some basic economics courses in their curricula.

There is another important component at work here. Business owners and managers are still people who have a conscience and very often lead their communities in the pursuit of improvements in the quality of life for everyone. This simple fact is proven again and again by simply looking at the volunteers who serve on the boards of directors of non-profit organizations, government advisory committees, school boards, and so on. As members of their respective communities, they have an investment in the elements making their communities a better place to live and work. Great communities are typically places with involved businesses, and their involvement is very often volunteer services and donations.

It has been stated that the quality of a civilization may be measured by the way it treats the least fortunate of its members. Persons with developmental disabilities involuntarily find themselves in this category. They neither elected to be born with the challenges they face, nor did they choose to engage in behaviors creating their situations. They are simply playing the hands dealt them by fate. Any one of us could have been in their situation if we did not have the good fortune to be born healthy. Business people often respond to this notion instinctively, although not necessarily without some information and understanding. It is our role as professionals, advocates, family members, or donors to help make the understanding possible.

It is when understanding occurs that the concept of mutual shared prosperity may be extended to persons with developmental disabilities. We must start with the acceptance of profits as being a requisite for business. Beyond that, if we can convince the business person that employing a person with disabilities should not diminish their profits, they may very well embrace the concept. The secret is to grasp the economics at work here and use them to advantage. A theory is only a good theory if it works in reality, so it is necessary to delve briefly into the mechanics of business accounting as it pertains to employment of people with disabilities.

All businesses provide some type of goods or services to their customers. In virtually every case they are in competition with other businesses for the same customers, and they must therefore maximize the value of their goods or services while minimizing their costs. Expenses can be either *fixed costs*, like rent or a mortgage, or *variable costs*, such as supplies or labor. Labor is a variable cost because it may go up or down as sales or work demands fluctuate. Persons with disabilities seeking to become employed become a variable cost to the business. The challenge is to demonstrate to the business that this cost is a worthwhile investment.

First, it is necessary to realize that not all businesses are structured in a way that this can be a cost-effective investment. Persons with developmental disabilities, by definition, are seldom able to acquire academic credentials or advanced technical training. The reality is that we must usually look at entry-level positions with minimal qualifications required. The good news about this is that these positions can be tremendously challenging and satisfying for the individuals we serve, and the employees can also advance with time. *The principle is to assist people in realizing their individualized potential, whatever that might be.* It is easy, and very wrong, to classify entry-level jobs as bad or insulting. Rather, they should be viewed as honorable, necessary work, and a way to start building a career. The author of this book started his career flipping hamburgers at a McDonald's while in high school. Later, he unloaded trucks as a college student and even worked for a time as a janitor. With additional skills and experience comes advancement, and that is exactly what we will try to accomplish with persons with developmental disabilities (hereinafter sometimes referred to as "clients" for the sake of brevity). We are all "clients" at times because we seek the services of professionals. The same rule applies here.

It has been well documented that the greatest source of job creation is the small business community. For this reason we will use small businesses as models, although the methods work equally well with large businesses. (There will be some additional insights included later in the discussion on "Corporate Job Development.") Far too many organized efforts to assist clients in becoming employed focus on government-subsidized contracts. There are two main problems with this. First, this tends to promote de facto segregation by isolating the workers out of mainstream employment. Second, it is tantamount to sentencing them to being non-competitive with other employees. This is demeaning, and it is a false assumption. Relying on government for employment tends to reinforce the stereotype of people with disabilities being unable to demonstrate their worth as employees on their own merits. This does not mean it should be totally excluded, only that it should be limited to a normal percentage of the overall mix of employers.

One of the costliest items for employers with entry-level positions is employee turnover. It is often estimated that each turnover of a position costs the employer anywhere from 10 to 33 percent of the position's annual wage. This is a very real, often massive expense for businesses and it is the key element in the argument for employing our clients. Many entry-level positions are taken by young workers who are far more likely to move on with the first opportunity. Others are taken by individuals with poor work habits and a history of repetitive job-hopping. Sadly, many others have substance-abuse problems, criminal histories, or other issues which employers dread. It is difficult enough to operate a business successfully without having to wonder whether employees will show up for work the next day. We have heard employers lamenting this state of affairs, and have called us saying, "Please send me someone who will show up and wants to work!" If a business is experiencing turnover rates for these jobs of 20, 50, or even 100 percent annually, this is fertile ground for job developing.

Persons with developmental disabilities have been able to demonstrate longevity in their employment. We have worked with many individuals who have been with the same employer for 5, 10, 15 years or more. As a result, it is not unusual for them to gain seniority and the accompanying status it confers. This simple fact can produce a level of self-esteem in our clients that is impossible to produce elsewhere. Very interesting and positive experiences spring from these situations. One of the more rewarding is to see one of our clients asked to train another new (non-disabled) employee. This produces massive self-esteem. It may be the first time that our client was on the teaching side of the table.

As a person with disabilities becomes a long-term employee, his or her skills tend to increase, earnings improve, responsibilities grow, and they achieve a level of parity with their peer employees that no typical social program could ever hope to achieve. Working alongside someone tends to become the greatest social equalizer. The person with a developmental disability tends to become a *person*, period. This rather remarkable phenomenon goes to the heart of the matter referred to earlier, in that the individual seeks acceptance as a person rather than as a word delineating some sort of diagnosis.

There are many other positive outcomes which are difficult to quantify but nevertheless quite real. Clients who work in teams with other employees who are not disabled simply have fewer problems in general. Intangible though they may be, these benefits are readily observable by any practitioner with knowledge of this population. Much of the reason for this comes from the psychological concept of "situational demand." Stated simply, this means that certain situations such as a workplace, with its inherent demands for performance, tend to raise the overall level of expectations for the individual. It is human nature to raise or lower performance in many areas according to the expectations in a given situation, and our clients are no different in this respect. We will return to this subject later when we discuss training methodologies. For now, it is enough to know that high expectations come from integrated settings with "normal" performance the standard. This, of course, means that living up to one's full potential is unlikely to occur in segregated work settings where expectations are invariably lower because the workers all have disabilities. Try as we might, we are unable to truly replicate the reality of a competitive business in these settings.

Let us look at an example from a purely financial perspective. A small business with 20 employees has three entry-level jobs. On average, they have been turning over every 12 months. This is an annual turnover rate of 100 percent! Assuming an average wage rate of $16,600, and a modest turnover cost of 15 percent, this results in a net cost to the employer of $7,470 annually. For most small businesses, this is a fairly significant amount of money. As the numbers of employees increase, this cost increases correspondingly. If we are able to match one of our clients to this job successfully, the potential exists to add this amount to the annual profits of the business each year. A major advantage for our clients is that they do tend to regard these positions as career jobs, rather than a short-term cash fix, and they tend to stay for years and years. Demonstrating these facts to employers provides a great incentive to hire. It must be pointed out here that it is true that our clients do typically require a longer period of time to learn the respective job. It is also true that they are more likely to have limitations on flexibility involving different jobs, or learning new skills. Nevertheless, these downsides are usually temporary and normally far outweighed by the savings in turnover expenses.

Here is a trick question used in training new staff who will do job developing. What is the average productivity of the non-disabled workers in a given business? The answers usually vary from 50 to 90 percent, but the correct answer is 100 percent. This is true because it is simply the output of all the workers divided by the number of workers. It has to be 100 percent. The individual workers, however, often vary quite dramatically. We have all had low-producing co-workers who irritate the rest of us. We have also envied those who seem to be able to get far more work done than just about everyone else. When their respective outputs are combined and averaged, it is inevitably 100 percent for that particular business.

This fact is important to understand because there are often assumptions made that our clients need to be able to produce at a 100 percent rate of "normal" output in order to compete for jobs. As we have just seen, this is clearly not the case. In a typical workplace with entry-level positions we would expect to find output percentages ranging from 60 or 70 percent to 150 percent or more. Amazingly, they are all employed and often at the same rate of pay. It is true that the workers at the lowest rates are sometimes replaced, but more often they get by because of the turnover problem. It is therefore true that a person who works slower than the average can nevertheless earn the prevailing wage for that job. Indeed, with time and practice their productivity tends to increase along with additional responsibilities. These facts argue very well for hiring our clients and letting them master their positions. Smart business managers can see this with some information and good references from other employers.

There are several distinct advantages to employers in hiring persons with disabilities. In supported employment, the "support" typically includes ongoing job coaching provided by a trained staff person. This means that many routine tasks, such as retraining for new job requirements, may be handled by the staff person. This can be a real time-saving for the employer. It may also include assisting in dealing with various personal issues that invariably occur with virtually all employees. Employers benefit from this assistance.

Another more intangible benefit often accrues which many employers would not predict. Over time, their other employees begin to appreciate the fact that they work for an employer who is contributing something very positive to their community. It is, indeed, very common for the employer to hear compliments about this fact and it ends up contributing to overall staff morale. This is obviously difficult to measure. Nevertheless, one of the best ways to capture it is to obtain recommendations from existing employers. Some of these are amazingly heartfelt and moving. A short video featuring testimonials is an incredibly effective tool in telling this story direct from employers who have experienced it. A packet of letters from existing employers is very powerful. A prospective employer is far more likely to believe this coming from a fellow employer than from us.

In typical job development efforts, a prospective employer will pose a variety of questions and concerns about the potential downsides of hiring a person who has a disability. Some of these will be presented here in a question and response format, with each typical response based on actual experiences.

- *Won't hiring this person increase the chances of workplace accidents, and increase my workers' compensation insurance?*

Our experience is that persons with disabilities do not increase the probability of accidents. In fact, our own experience rating modification is well below average. (An "experience rating modification" is a worker's compensation score rating the frequency of accidents in a particular business compared to other businesses in that industry. "Below average" is good, meaning that the frequency of accidents is less than would normally be expected. This score is then used to decrease or increase the cost of the insurance correspondingly.)

• *What if this person does not work out and we have to fire her? Won't we get sued for discrimination?*

We guarantee, in writing if you would like, that we will do everything in our power to prevent that from happening. In fact, if you are unhappy with the employee for any reason we will immediately assist you in ending the employment relationship. We will then work to find that person a different job. We will also commit to defending your decision if needed. With our role as advocates for persons with disabilities, this carries enormous weight. We have never had this occur with one of our employees, and we would never expect this to happen. Instead, we would ask that we could be permitted to refer another person for you to consider in the hope that we would find a better match for this position. Our main desire is to have both the employer and the employee satisfied with the situation. (Note: employers love this, and it helps with placing the next person when needed.)

• *What if this person is just too slow and this increases my labor costs?*

Our experience has been that, after an initial period of our individualized training, the performance tends to fall within very acceptable rates. In many cases, it can exceed that of non-disabled workers. However, if the person's performance continues at a less than acceptable rate we do have a mechanism to deal with this. We can assist you in obtaining a special certificate allowing a wage less than the normal minimum. We can provide productivity measurements and the pay rate can be adjusted to match actual performance. (Note: this is actually quite rare. In fact, the vast majority of clients earn at or above minimum-wage levels. More on this later.)

- *Our customers may not be used to being around people with disabilities, and may complain.*

Our experience has been that this virtually never happens. Instead, it is very common to hear of compliments from customers. We have had a number of clients receive awards for exemplary customer service. One supermarket chain utilizes secret shoppers, and a client there has received regional awards for the best customer service of any employee in the store.

- *What if a disciplinary action has to be taken? How would we be able to deal with that?*

First, we strongly recommend that employees with disabilities follow the same policies as any other employee, and that (in general) they are held to the same standards of performance. Further, they should be held accountable the same as anyone else. If assistance is needed in explaining a disciplinary action we will be happy to provide it.

Interestingly, we often find ourselves recommending a disciplinary action before the employer when there is a serious performance issue. They do sometimes have a tendency to allow too much leeway, and we discourage this. It may seem kind in the short term, but it can create unrealistic expectations and do great harm in the long run.

3

*U*nderstanding Job Success

Let us begin with a definition. *Job success means the client likes the job, the employer likes having the client as an employee, and the job continues for a minimum of six months.* Anything less should not be considered a success because there is too much time and money involved to keep repeating the process. A good placement procedure is an investment, not a quick statistic.

There is a tendency for inexperienced job developers to try to short-cut the placement process. This occurs because they desire to see their client placed and on a job, as if that alone denoted success. It also occurs because they do not understand why jobs are lost, or that job retention is the real measure of success. Instead, they tend to engage in wishful thinking that all that is needed is a job and everything else will miraculously take care of itself. This is not the case.

A prevailing view is that if the client can handle the technical requirements of a job he or she will be successful. As a result, a great deal of time and effort is expended toward dealing with the mechanics of the job in question. However, *a fundamental principle of job success is the understanding that most job losses are caused by problems in the social, rather than technical, arena of workplaces.* In other words, our clients can often master the necessary technical requirements much better than they can master the social requirements. These are far more difficult to master, and for a variety of reasons.

Most of the rest of us (the "non-disabled") have had a far broader range of social experiences. Typically, we have learned many of the social nuances and mores through thousands of trials and errors, starting with childhood. As we progressed into adulthood, our experiences became more sophisticated and complex. A social faux pas was often met with correction, or consequences in one form or another, and we gradually integrated these refined expectations into our behavioral repertoire. If, for example, we simply failed to meet basic expectations like good attendance in our first entry-level job, we may have been summarily fired. This sort of experience stays with us forever, and shapes our future reactions to similar situations. These are often referred to as "natural consequences."

Many of our clients have had far more limited experiences. Some have been denied opportunities to mingle socially and learn what is expected in the way we did. Some have been excessively sheltered out of concern for their safety, or perhaps the safety of others. Sometimes family members feel guilty about the person's disability and overcompensate through coddling behavior. Normal situations like establishing relationships with the opposite sex may have been discouraged, repressed, or denied entirely. Many have suffered abuse or neglect. In far too many cases clients have been treated as children and denied the opportunity to assume responsibility for the choices they make. Some educational programs create false or distorted realities wherein students are led to believe that their actions are not connected to real consequences. In effect, the absence of choice is synonymous with the lack of understanding of natural consequences. Therefore, it should come as no surprise that their abstract reasoning required for understanding complex social constructs is often diminished. In fact, much of our current socialization of persons with developmental disabilities actually exacerbates their challenges, and leaves them even less prepared to take on independence. Clearly, these issues pose significant challenges but they can be ameliorated with effective strategies.

A primary premise in various theories of management and quality assurance is that the right outcome will follow the right process. Knowing a good strategy is not enough to produce a good outcome. Rather, the right strategies employing the right process have the greatest likelihood of success. The very first step in this process is establishing consensus on the goal itself. This may seem self-evident, but it is most assuredly not the case.

For the vast majority of individuals with developmental disabilities, there are usually a number of "stakeholders" involved. These are the people who ultimately make up the individual's support team. They may be family members, agents of funding sources, other service providers, medical professionals, advocates, and so on. Each will bring a unique perspective to a given situation. If these stakeholders are at odds when it comes to the client's employment, success becomes almost impossible. Consensus on the goal of job placement is absolutely critical. This does not necessarily mean 100 percent agreement, but it does require unanimous support of the goal once it has been established. Reaching consensus requires leadership, and it often provides an opportunity to surface underlying counterproductive assumptions. It should also be made clear that only the job placement staff should have contact with the employer. Team meetings should never occur at the place of employment.

As discussed above, many of our clients have had difficult histories in addition to dealing with their disabilities. As we attempt to develop a consensus on a goal for employment, many of these difficulties begin to emerge. We tend to see repetitions of behaviors, which society might deem "deviant" or unacceptable, followed by either the absence of normal consequences or a rationalization of the problem behavior. Although not all need to be confronted by the job development professional, they do need to be recognized and assimilated into the planning process. There are two methods for getting at these.

The first method is a planning session with all the key stakeholders present. It should be a given that the client is at the center of this process and ultimately makes the final decision. However, this understanding is not always present with all participants, especially if they have been in the role of decision-maker in the past. Our responsibility is to encourage and reinforce that "self-directed" decision-making by the client to the greatest extent feasible. In the case where a court has appointed someone as a guardian for the individual, this obviously must be respected but without diminishing the individual's dignity or importance.

This planning session, like all well-planned meetings, should have a clearly stated purpose, a skilled facilitator, and some basic ground rules so that inappropriate domination of the meeting is controlled. The purpose of the meeting is to establish the employment goal for the individual.

The other method of establishing the goal is to work independently with the stakeholders, then present a goal to them for acceptance. Each method has advantages and disadvantages, and should be selected as one chooses the right tool for a job.

The first step is to gain a basic understanding of the client.

4

*U*nderstanding the Client

The process of understanding the client is yet another example of something that may at first seem simple but is actually quite complex. In fact, it should be approached somewhat as a detective would go about solving a mystery. We must start with the premise that each individual is unique, with a unique combination of talents and challenges influenced by a unique set of experiences. It is a common and deadly error to begin by making assumptions about the person, and even the most experienced job developer must guard against doing this. Further, as the mystery progresses we must consistently guard against coming to conclusions prematurely. Instead, we aim for "the light bulb" effect (to be discussed later).

Step 1: Research

Research begins with studying any and all documentation available. Some of this may be useful, some may be misleading, and some may be dangerously wrong. In any event, it should be utilized to generate a general sense of how the client managed to get to where he or she is now. This is the time to start taking notes on items to be remembered. These notes should be continued through each step, and will serve as a guide for answering questions, resolving contradictions, and establishing facts. All good detectives take notes as they conduct their investigations, and we need to follow their example. There are sometimes great volumes of background information available, and care must be taken to use good judgment on how much of this is relevant and useful. For example, extensive medical histories may be summarized using more recent records.

Here is the operative principle for guiding all research activity: *All stakeholders have a perspective, but no single perspective is sufficient alone.* The researcher has the challenge of sifting through the perspectives, confronting any apparent contradictions, and generating a new and more comprehensive understanding of the client.

The notion of "contradictions" may at first seem confusing, but it is actually quite common for these to show up during research. For example, we might find evidence of a prescription for a medication associated with control of seizures but no mention of a corresponding diagnosis. There could be a history of arrests in one file and a statement claiming there is no such history in another. There might be a reference to living independently for an extended period of time contrasted with an order of guardianship predicated on the inability of the client to care for him- or herself. Each of these may be factual in its own context, but each generates a need to fully understand how and why this can be so. The resulting notes are later used as a guide for discussion during interviews.

The area often generating the most discrepancies involves employment skills, history, and prospects. Regardless of the perspective being researched, objective facts are often victims of emotion, professional defensiveness, or selective inclusion. A television detective was once famous for demanding "just the facts, ma'am," and this should be our objective here. There is a time and place for opinions and conclusions, but it is not during the research phase.

Here is a classic example. A young adult, several years out of school, is referred for assistance in finding a job. The information provided speaks of how successful the person has been at a series of jobs, what amazing skills he has, and how he just kept moving on "to get a better job." As we research these jobs, however, we discover that several were unpaid volunteer jobs, one was only one hour per week, and the last one ended in termination after three days. The lesson here is that the devil is indeed in the detail, and the details must be known. It is amazing how often this sort of scene repeats itself, and we must get past the surface layer if we are going to be able to move on to a successful job placement.

Reviewing documentation should also generate notes about what other kinds of information should be obtained. For example, if a person has received job development services previously, it is very helpful to request that history. A recent school program may contain very relevant information. Medical information can be difficult to obtain or understand, but a summary of hospitalizations, treatments, prescriptions, or vulnerabilities may be critical to the job placement planning process. A medical consultation may be needed to facilitate this part of the research.

Another difficult area to research is behavioral challenges. There are a number of reasons for this. First, the person or organization referring the client sometimes withholds certain facts out of fear that the individual will not be accepted as a client. (Although this is possible, judgment should normally be withheld at this point in the process.) It is also true that a behavioral challenge may well have been limited to a particular context, environment, or personal interaction. Very often a change in the environment changes the behavior.

Perhaps the most critical area to research is criminal history. Like behavioral challenges, many issues change with a different environment. Nevertheless, it is always important to know the facts at the beginning of the placement process. The worst time to find out something of this nature is when a person is ready to be placed into employment or is already doing the job. A criminal history, in and of itself, by no means disqualifies a person for employment. Rather, it may create certain limitations, job parameters, or support requirements.

If there is a criminal history it must receive serious consideration. Fortunately, these situations are relatively rare but the details of the offense must be known before any plan for placement can be started. The job developer must know exactly what happened if a problem with the placement is to be prevented. Reviewing this may be uncomfortable for the client and family, but denial of the facts is worse. In the vast majority of cases there is still an employment situation that is quite feasible. Full disclosure is the only acceptable way to proceed, and this means disclosing (with prior consent) the history to a prospective employer. While it is true that some employers may pass on hiring the person because of this fact, it is far worse for the employer to discover it on their own later on. The worst situation imaginable is for a similar offense to occur on the job when disclosure was inappropriately withheld. In this situation, employers have sometimes successfully sued the organization which placed the individual. This employer will invariably avoid hiring other persons referred by the same organization.

Step 2: Interviews

Detectives consider an interview as a "conversation with a purpose." Our purpose for an interview is to gain an understanding of the interviewee's perspective. We also must remember that each interviewee has only a piece of the broader perspective we seek. It brings to mind a story of a group of people, all visually impaired, who came upon an elephant. Each touched a part of the animal and announced to his companions what he had discovered. Each had a different part, of course, and each was completely accurate in his description of the trunk, tail, leg, and so on. None, however, had a true or complete assessment of the object of their discussion. Only by comparing and contrasting their descriptions could a complete picture emerge. So it is with interviews about our client. We start with the person in question.

If any significant progress is to be realized we must put ourselves into the shoes of our client, as best we can, and grasp the concept that we are asking them to place their trust in us. At risk is the potential of a new, potentially life-changing job. Something this significant invariably generates anxiety and occasionally outright fear. It is human nature to have this reaction to a major change, and we must keep this thought in mind each step of the way. The principle governing our efforts, therefore, is: *A major change like a new job first requires trust, and the trust must be earned.*

There are far too many people who enter social services work laboring under the illusion that they will ride in as a kind of hero on a white horse and start saving people. The reality is that most of us usually have our own problems. The mere fact that we have ended up in a position with the responsibility of assisting a client in obtaining employment is meaningless when it comes to determining their willingness to trust us. We have to earn it first. If there is one particular skill our clients seem to have in abundance, it is the ability to sense quickly who it is they do not like.

Trust is intangible, difficult to measure, hard to define, and impossible to package. Somewhere down the road, when we have completed much of our job placement process, we will probably need to ask someone to do something they might not feel comfortable doing. When this occurs, the determining variable will probably be the presence (or absence) of trust. Further, it will usually require trust from the client, his or her family, the prospective employer, and other significant stakeholders. Gaining trust is easier said than done.

First and foremost, we must realize that trust requires an investment of time. Quick-fix solutions are a lot like quick and easy job placements in that they usually do not last. Solid investments over time produce solid results, and that should be the way to approach this piece of the puzzle. Establishing trust depends on empathy, quality communication, technical competence, and follow-through.

Empathy is simple enough in that we merely need to be able to have an understanding of what the other person is feeling. It is the sort of thing that cannot be taught. We either have it or not, and without it there is no point in pursuing a career working with people who have severe disabilities.

Quality communication means that we are truthful, relay information without delay, and ensure that the message intended is the message received.

Technical competence means having the requisite skills for the task at hand, and exercising sound judgment in problem-solving. Occasionally we see "professionals" who are the equivalent of a one-trick pony. Every new client they encounter is simply a repetition of a past client rather than a new, fresh, individualized challenge, and every problem gets the same tool selected as a would-be solution.

Last, and far from least, is *follow-through*. In the fields of rehabilitation and related social services there seems to be an institutionalized tolerance for a systemic lack of follow-through on responsibilities. There are probably numerous rationalizations for this, but none are convincing. We have all heard the excuses ranging from "I was just too busy" to "It's not my job," and even worse attempts to avoid responsibility. Examples of this range from failure to return telephone calls promptly to just ignoring vital work that needs to be done without delay. In most businesses this sort of poor performance is seldom tolerated for long because it causes rather immediate financial consequences. However, in government-funded work and even some non-profit organizations there may be a great distance between professional apathy and real consequences. For our purposes, follow-through on commitments is absolutely essential to establishing trust. The old saying about "do not promise more than you can deliver, and deliver more than you promise" is a great one to remember here.

Let us now return to the interview with our new client. This is our first step in establishing trust, and the only way to begin to understand how this individual sees the world. This is not a place for being judgmental or critical in any way whatsoever. It is an opportunity to let the person tell you all about him- or herself, from historical information to family and friends, educational experiences, employment experiences, hobbies, likes, dislikes, achievements, disappointments, and whatever else comes into their mind. A common and often fatal error made by inept job developers is to focus exclusively on employment-related information. This is just wrong. It is absolutely vital to hear what is important to clients, what they value, what they dislike, who they dislike and why, and how they have come to these conclusions. It does not mean that these views are set in stone and may never be influenced, but it does define what problems may reside in these views and what issues might need to be addressed before a job placement plan can be developed.

Let us look at an example. Our new client tells us he wants to work with computers, and that he spends several hours each day "working with computers." This preference is sometimes reinforced by a family member. However, additional inquiries reveal that "working with computers" actually means that the person enjoys "surfing" the internet and playing games. This is just not a skill with real value in the labor market. It should be considered in the same vein as a desire to be a nuclear physicist. We term these "unrealistic expectations," and they will eventually require some compassionate counseling about the realities of employment.

Other interviewees may also harbor unrealistic expectations. The important thing is to listen carefully and withhold judgment until a comprehensive understanding of the client is realized. Far more important, at this stage, is to pursue abilities which may not be readily apparent. For example, we may learn that our client has a passion for taking mechanical things apart. There are actually jobs requiring this kind of skill. There may be a latent talent for artistic activities, such as arranging things in an esthetically pleasing way. Someone who is naturally friendly or gregarious may be able to use this to advantage in the right kind of job. There are many, many ways that a person may have unusual abilities with value in the right work environment. Our task is to ferret these out through interviews with a representative variety of informed stakeholders. At the same time we keep taking notes so that we will have the necessary ingredients to resolve any apparent discrepancies. This occurs during a part of the process we term "cross-referencing."

Step 3: Cross-referencing

"Cross-referencing" means taking all the information we have gathered and using it to surface contradictions or discrepancies. If there are glaring oppositional views of the client's skills or challenges it is often wise to review these as a complete team working together. Sometimes the mere presence of informed people in the same room at the same time may help resolve these issues, but a facilitated discussion with a skilled leader is critical. Our objective here is to determine what we can agree on, and then systematically discuss areas of conflict with the intent to gain consensus. It can be difficult, and this is why trust is so important, but it can be done and it is critically important.

In other cases the information comes in relatively consistently and a team planning session as described above may not be necessary. This is a judgment call, and the skilled professional will choose the correct tool at the right time. *In all cases it is essential to arrive at a realistic, achievable, and supportable goal. If this is not achieved, absolutely no job development of any kind should occur.* Rather, it will be necessary to back up and go through some of the previous steps in an effort to gain consensus. It may, in rare cases, be necessary to delay the process while some of the stakeholders take additional time to process information contrary to their own beliefs.

Step 4: The light bulb moment

We use the analogy of a light bulb coming on to describe the moment at which we finally "get it." In other words, we have managed to come to a point where we believe we now know this client well enough that we will not be surprised in any significant way once we have placed him or her into a job. This is easier said than done, and experience will be a great shaper of this event. Nevertheless, most of the obvious job-killing surprises are, in fact, discoverable if we ask the right questions and resolve discrepancies to our satisfaction. We must overcome the temptation to make a quick job placement while we patiently learn about our client. It is only when we believe there is nothing else of consequence to be learned that we are able to say the light bulb has come on, and we are ready to begin job development.

5

*The Job Development Plan

This is the final step required before any job developing activity occurs. The *job development plan* is a written summary of the key parameters of the job we will seek, a summary of the skills and challenges our client presents, and a summary of the strategy we will employ in the search. In no way should it be construed merely as a "form" which must be filled out. It is a plan which, when signed by the stakeholders, serves as a compass in our search as well as a de facto license to pursue the job on our client's behalf. We will list the essential ingredients as a basis for developing a template, but the important thing to remember is that these are all critical elements requiring consideration. They are not just lines on a form to be completed as some sort of exercise. Each and every one of these items has, in fact, created a job loss when it was ignored. This is why they are included here.

Client data

Just the usual name, address, and contact information.

Geographic area

This should be as specific as possible, and should delineate what area is accessible by the client on a continuing basis. There are a host of factors at play, including the availability of public transportation systems, the mobility and physical health of the client, his or her safety in the community at large, the availability of alternative modes such as car pools or relatives, and so on.

Days and times available

When we deal with clients who have limited or no employment experience there is a tendency to generalize that almost any days and times would be acceptable for employment. The reality is that this is virtually never the case. In fact, most people have some established routines or priorities that are near and dear to them. These could be things like church activities, sporting events, Special Olympics, clubs, and others. It is absolutely essential that these kinds of things are known about and accounted for in the job development plan. Sometimes it is necessary for the client to make tough choices about what is more important—a job or a personal pursuit. This is something we all do in life, and we need to respect the dignity involved in sorting these things out and prioritizing them. It may be necessary for the client to confront some difficult but necessary choices with the support of the team.

Minimum and maximum earnings

This is a deceptively simple component. First, the minimum earnings requirement means that we must determine the amount the client will need to meet existing obligations and expenses. Sometimes these are low and that makes it easy. In other cases there are very real considerations such as rent, food, utilities, and so forth, which must be factored in. If the job eventually offered is unable to meet these expectations, the job development efforts will have been wasted.

The maximum amount desired may seem like an absurd issue at first glance, but in many cases there are benefits (such as Social Security, Supplementary Security Income [SSI], or rent subsidy eligibility) that will be threatened by earnings over certain amounts. These issues need to be explored ahead of time so that there are no disruptive disqualifications for much-needed benefits. The minimum and maximum amounts desired should be stated clearly, and converted to a desired range of both compensation and the amount of time routinely scheduled for work.

Abilities which will help to secure employment

These are the talents, skills, assets, advantages, and motivations which we will be able to present to a prospective employer. There is an old sales technique that is sometimes referred to as "sell the sizzle." This means that we present the aspects of the person which stand out and help to differentiate him or her from other applicants. Do not exaggerate or misrepresent. Rather, use that which is there combined with judgment and a respect for the marketing strategy of knowing your customer and your client. Read more on this in Chapter 6.

Challenges

If there were no challenges present the client would already be employed, so we should simply take it as a given that there will be some challenges and move on. It does not help matters to deny that they exist, or rationalize them, or just avoid talking about them. Employers know that virtually all of their prospective employees will present some challenges. They will differ from employee to employee, but they will still exist. They also realize that someone who has support staff has to have even greater challenges. The important thing here is that many of our clients will present challenges which are more acceptable than others, and not that they will not have any at all. By being candid with employers, we help to establish trust with them. Besides, any challenges present will emerge over time anyway.

Our strategy needs to accept the challenges that exist, and then establish a means of dealing with them successfully. First and foremost, we need to formalize a plan capitalizing on the client's abilities while avoiding the more difficult challenges. Here is an example. If the person has an eating disorder, placement in a food service position would be a fundamental error. If this sounds way too obvious, rest assured it is based on a real experience in which the client was simply not known well enough prior to job develop-ment. The light bulb never came on. The job was lost, and all the job development and training time was wasted. The employer was upset, the client was unhappy, and a lot of effort went down the drain. There are countless other examples, but the point is that these challenges need to be understood and acknowledged in the job development plan.

Description of the successful job

This part is a bit like sports psychology, wherein success is envi-sioned before play begins. It means we need to be able to visualize what the successful job situation might look like. The actual job *functions* are usually not as important as many of the social and environmental aspects of the job. The client may dislike big, noisy environments, for example, or workplaces with strong odors. Sometimes the presence of dirt can make a job unsatisfactory. In the majority of cases the social skills expectations will be a critical variable. A client with poor hygiene skills is doomed to failure in a professional office building, but may do very well in some factory settings. Someone who is extremely sensitive will wilt under a loud, insensitive supervisor, but may thrive with a gentle, com-passionate supervisor. (Yes, they actually do exist!) If a successful work situation cannot be envisioned, there is additional work to be done. This might include some "work experience" situations on a short, temporary basis, where the individual volunteers for a few days. This is one way to see how he or she will react in some new environments. In the end, we should be able to describe in a few sentences what this successful work situation looks like.

Transportation

The overwhelming majority of individuals with developmental disabilities do not drive. Other methods of getting to and from work on a sustained basis are required. This topic should be discussed openly and thoroughly, with all the options being reviewed. Occasionally a job is located within walking distance of the client's home but that is rare. Sometimes riding a bike to work is viable, or public transportation, or even special transportation with some kind of subsidy involved. Alternatives such as car-pooling or ride-sharing with co-workers should also be explored. Family members or friends may be options. Networking, posting an advertisement, or reviewing advertisments posted at an employer's premises may also sometimes provide a solution. Safety must always be factored in of course, but there are many ways of ensuring this with good discussion and planning. The main point is that it is not possible to have job success if there is no reliable means of getting to and from work.

The goal

The goal is a simple, clear statement describing, with the greatest specificity possible, what the desired outcome is. We need, as the client who will be employed and the team of supportive people who will assist them, to arrive at consensus on this goal or we will fail. It is not essential to have 100 percent agreement but it is essential to have 100 percent support for the goal.

Here are a few examples of what a job goal might look like.

"20–25 hour per week job as sub-assembler in a light manu-facturing plant in southeast…"

"30–35 hours per week including evenings and weekends, as server in a family-style restaurant within three miles of home."

"Part-time job as greeter at Wal-Mart."

"Afternoon/evenings-only work at a supermarket as courtesy clerk."

"Full-time job in data entry in a professional office building."

All goals need to be made within the context of the local job market. This is yet another reason why the involvement of stakeholders as a team effort may be instrumental in shaping a realistic goal.

Job development strategy

The job development strategy is the process of writing down what we will do, who will do it, and when we will do it, in an effort to achieve the established goal. This strategy may be written as a series of "objectives" which will lead to the established goal. *A key principle here is that the client and key stakeholders must also establish ownership in helping to achieve the goal.* There needs to be investment of time, effort, and sometimes even some money to establish any ownership of the desired outcome. It is truly a team effort, and it is also true that the team can help to celebrate success when the goal is achieved, solve problems when they arise, or commiserate when a job is lost. It is infinitely better to approach this as a team than to struggle as a single person in the role of job developer.

One of the best ways that team members can be involved is through networking. Everyone knows people who are employed in various businesses, and each of them may be contacted as a means of networking. The majority of jobs found for persons with developmental disabilities are not advertised like many other jobs. Instead, they are developed through business and personal contacts. Using team members to expand the range and reach of these contacts is vital.

Team members may also assume responsibilities such as training a client how to use public transportation, utilize vending machines, order a taxi, cash a check, dress for interviews, and so on. This list is endless, and should be developed based on the individual's needs. The important thing is to write down the responsibilities so that everyone knows exactly what is expected of them.

This list should include the client as well. Some responsibilities, for example, might include cutting out one or two employment advertisments which seem like feasible options, buying a new set of clothes for interviews, or visiting a list of businesses and observing people at work to get a sense of what goes on there.

It usually helps to develop a resumé, and the job developer should take on this task. Even someone with no work history can have a helpful resumé. Most entry-level jobs have supervisors who are familiar with inexperienced workers. It should be accurate, even if it is brief, and should highlight some of the strengths described earlier.

The job developer's responsibilities and actions should be listed in the order they need to be done. In addition to developing a resumé, they may include arranging for practice interviews with someone unfamiliar to the client. Sometimes videotaping these interviews and then reviewing them with the client can help them to see what needs to be improved. Practice makes perfect, so doing multiple practice interviews is excellent procedure.

Visiting friendly employers is also a good strategy. Because so many of our clients have very limited experience, they may have no idea what we are talking about when we mention a certain kind of employment. These visits should be strictly for the experience of learning about the different kinds of work environments that exist, and not as a means of "marketing" the client.

Experience is the operative word in this equation. We cannot emphasize enough how important it is for the client to actually experience real job situations, even if these experiences are only ten minutes long. Using only words to describe a job situation completely outside of a person's realm of experiences is simply inadequate for them to gain true understanding.

Team signatures

It is vital that all team members sign the job development plan when it is written. Team members should then receive a copy so that everyone understands clearly what the goal is and who will be doing what. Another important reason is that later on, when a real job opportunity is developed, it can help deal with any last-minute hesitation which sometimes occurs. A new job is a huge change, and the client or team members, or both, may feel threatened when it becomes an imminent possibility. The signed job development plan can be very useful in these situations. The job developer can review the process, the discussions, the team consensus, and all the work done to make the job possible. Very often this review can help assuage doubts or fears. In any event, no job developing effort should occur until the job development plan is completed and signed. This prevents a lot of wasted time, effort, and ultimately money.

Sample Placement Plan

1. Client data

John Smith
1234 North Rose Street
Springfield

2. Geographic area

Downtown Springfield, North to Highway 222, near bus lines

3. Days and times available

Preferred days are Monday through Friday. Saturdays would be acceptable for the right job, but are not preferred because of Special Olympics practice. John is not available to work on Sundays.
John is a late riser and has had difficulties with early morning jobs. It would be best if the job started between 10:00a.m. and noon. Late afternoons and early evenings are acceptable, but arrangements would need to be made for special transportation after 8:00p.m.

4. Minimum and maximum earnings

John has an apartment, and he needs a total of $1,250 per month for all his expenses. With a $600 Supplementary Security Income check, he needs at least $650 per month in earnings. He also needs to stay under about $920 in earnings so he does not jeopardize his eligibility for benefits including his health insurance card.

5. Abilities which will help secure employment

John is very dependable the vast majority of the time. He shows up for work unless he is sick or has made previous arrangements to be absent. He has a wonderful personality and is always well-liked by supervisors and co-workers. Once he has thoroughly learned how to do a job, he continues to do it well for a long time. He is known for his smile and his cheerful personality. He has a very comitted work ethic. He receives some residential support services. His sister and brother live in the vicinity and are very supportive of the job placement effort.

6. Challenges

John does not read or write beyond a second grade level, so this will limit job opportunities. He does not drive and will need to rely on bus services or be within a mile or so of a job so he can walk or ride his bike. He will need assistance reading work schedules or completing time sheets. He also takes a medication at midday, and would need an opportunity to do this at work. John is a steady worker but is not particularly fast at anything. Sometimes John forgets to put on clean clothes in the morning.

7. Description of the successful job

A successful job for John would be one where he could use his personality to an advantage. There would be lots of interaction with people but without technical skills being necessary. John likes to have some physical activity so this would be a good element. The job should not require proficiency in math, reading, or writing.

8. Transportation

Primary transportation will be public transit, although if the job is less than a mile from home John will probably walk to work on nice days. Large, busy intersections are difficult for him so he would prefer to be able to avoid them on his route. If the weather is very bad his sister, who lives nearby, could provide a ride for him on occasion.

9. The goal

A customer service job, such as a courtesy clerk, in a large retail market, 20–25 hours per week. Monday through Saturday between 10:00a.m. and 7:00p.m. are good hours for him to work. A patient supervisor would be desirable, and an understanding of John's need to take medication during his shift.

10. Job development strategy

Action	By When	Responsibility
Develop resume and application information	Sept. 10	John, Employment Specialist
Develop a morning task reminder for clothes	Sept. 12	John, sister
Submit application to employment office	Sept. 15	John, Employment Specialist
Visit 6 retail markets for job observation	Sept. 20	John, Employment Specialist
Contact 10 employees of retail markets	Sept. 23	Sister, Employment Specialist, brother, friend
Submit applications to all markets in area	Sept. 30	John, Employment Specialist
Conduct 3 practice interviews	Sept. 30	John, Employment Specialist
Follow-up calls to markets	Oct. 7	Employment Specialist

11. Team signatures

John Smith _____

Sarah Smith (sister) _____

Robert Smith (brother) _____

Representative of funding source_____

Residential support staff _____

Employment Specialist _____

6

*I*ndividual Job Development

There are two basic approaches to job development: individual and corporate. In individual job development we have a specific client and we are looking for a certain type of job for him or her. In corporate job development, we are working with an employer whom we hope may have job opportunities that we may be able to use in the future. Corporate job development will be discussed in Chapter 7.

Once the job development plan has been finalized, we can begin by working on the objectives described earlier. One of the roles of the job developer during this period is to communicate with all the team members, facilitate progress, and coordinate responsibilities. The other main task is developing job opportunities. Some of the more traditional methods include the obvious employment advertisements in newspapers and online, employment office job postings, and word-of-mouth tips. Although these should definitely be included, more jobs for our clients are found using non-traditional methods.

Three degrees of separation

The first of these is called the "Three Degrees of Separation" method. We start by identifying a potential employer. Then we

research the employer using websites, business association list-
ings, and other internet searches to find the names of owners or
managers. It is best to identify the top decision-making people
at the outset. Once we know whom it is we wish to contact, we
look for an intermediary who can arrange an introduction. These
can almost always be found if we look hard enough. Boards of
directors, other employers, staff, family members, and others can
be approached to assist us in becoming acquainted. That, in effect,
is all we are really requesting here. We use this "back door" approach because the person guarding the "front door" has often
been trained to resist calls of this nature. Receptionists, human re-
source staff, and others may simply state there are no jobs available
and end the search immediately. This is why getting to the chief
executive officer (CEO), owner, or another top decision-maker is
vital. Experience has demonstrated that successful job development often hinges on the ability to make the right connection,
using a third-party intermediary, and having that person make the
introduction. Business is really quite personal in this way.

The marketing concept

Marketing is a vast subject, but for our purpose we will edit it down
to a single basic concept. We start with the premise that we need
to develop a solid understanding of what our customer needs and
wants before we even consider if we have something that might fit.
In this context, the customer is the potential employer. It is usually
a fatal business error to march in and try to sell something before
gaining an understanding of the customer first. This is why we
arrange a meeting, at the employer's business site, at a time when
it is convenient for them, and with no preconceptions of where it
may lead.

First, we should have completed some good research on the
employer so that we are at least basically familiar with their products, services, size, locations, and other similar fundamental facts.
A very important element to elicit is the company philosophy

or mission statement. Coming into the meeting thus informed demonstrates professionalism. Arriving without doing this basic research indicates amateurism.

Our meeting should lean toward the informal side since we really have no formal agenda at this point. We should briefly explain what we do but without creating an impression we are going to push for any kind of action on the part of the company. It is best to ask a lot of questions about the business operations and let the principal guide the discussion. Eventually the topic of employees will work its way in, and this is the time to ask about the workforce in general. Eventually, we should be able to get some ideas about their skill requirements, turnover rates, kinds of jobs, and any issues that are brought up by the employer. It can be very surprising to discover how willing they are to talk about their business, but this is actually a fairly normal expression of human nature. Because of this willingness, it is often possible to get permission for a tour of the business. This is the most valuable part of the meeting.

During the tour we should remain aware of time and make a point to not overstay our welcome. Observing employees on the job is the best way to ascertain if there is potential for one of our clients. Asking more questions during this phase is very important because this will help in understanding this potential customer. In some cases there will be opportunities to provide some information about experience with other employers who may have dealt with some of the same kinds of issues.

The end of the meeting really depends on what the employer presented and what, if any, interest is expressed in what we might have to offer. If there were no indications that potential exists no action should be suggested. Rather, a sincere "thank you" for the opportunity to learn about the business and the time spent is all that is appropriate. Later, some notes about this employer and the jobs observed should be made as part of an employer database.

In some cases there will be an invitation to explore further. This is particularly true for employers with entry-level positions or high turnover rates, or both. It is very important to avoid any promises or commitments at this point, but rather to express interest in researching to determine if we might have an appropriate prospect. If there is an interest, it is critical to respond without delay.

Job carving

"Job carving" is an excellent way to restructure existing job functions to create a position for one of our clients. Many businesses, especially smaller ones, have to combine higher-level tasks with entry-level tasks to keep employees busy. While this makes sense at first glance, there is often a better way to organize these functions to improve productivity and reduce costs. This happens through a process referred to as "job carving."

Before any attempt at job carving can occur it is necessary to have a good understanding of the existing jobs and functions themselves. This is why the market concept and tours are so important. We begin by analyzing the functions and making notes about the amounts of time spent in differing levels of skill requirements. A hypothetical case study might best illustrate this process.

ABC Company has 20 employees. Of these, one is the owner, one is the bookkeeper, three are sales representatives, four are office staff, and the others work in shipping and receiving. We can usually eliminate all but the office staff and shipping or receiving employees in our considerations. Looking at these jobs we discover that one office staff member spends 30 minutes each day sorting mail. Another spends 15 minutes per day shredding old documents. A shipping person is assigned to restroom janitorial duty for about 30 minutes each day. Another has a very tedious job in entering receiving document numbers into a database each morning for about 90 minutes. What they all have in common is that they dislike these particular parts of their jobs and would prefer to be doing the higher skill level work they were hired (and are paid) to do. Needless to say, the employer is paying a premium in wages to get these tasks done but "someone has to do it" so it continues. Concurrently, as is almost always the case, other important work gets pushed aside, delayed, or performed in a less than ideal fashion. This is an opportunity for some job carving.

In this case we might propose to the employer that a part-time job could be carved from some of these duties. It could lead to a job description including the data entry, mail sorting, shredding, and restroom cleaning. Combined, they may add up to 2.5 hours on these functions. The real cost to the employer may be determined by calculating the employees' respective wages (and benefits) for this amount of time. Even if our client starts at a minimum wage level and requires 4.5 hours to complete the same work, the employer will usually save a fair amount of money. In addition, the other employees will be freed up to do work they are particularly qualified for and will add to the overall productivity of the business. They will also, in all probability, be greatly relieved they no longer have to do the jobs they dislike. Our client may then be presented with a challenging job, a start on a career path, and an opportunity to be a part of a real business and have real responsibilities. The end result is that there is now a great job for our client, where before there was no job with that description, no opening, no advertising, and no prospect. The employer has decreased costs, improved productivity, and in all likelihood improved morale.

References

References are a vital tool for working with prospective employers. A starting place is a list of existing employers with successful job placements. This should contain basic contact information, telephone numbers, type of job, and tenure of the employee(s). We can say all we like about how well it works to hire a person with a disability, but another employer's statement will carry infinitely more weight.

An even better tool for this purpose is a short DVD featuring endorsements from existing employers and brief shots of the worker doing the job in question. Employers tend to be more will-ing to do this than we might expect, and the workers usually love having someone take this kind of special interest in what they do. DVDs are not terribly expensive to produce and they tell the story in a way that words alone cannot match.

Job matching

The secret ingredient in job placement is job matching. All the best efforts will be for naught if there is not a deliberate and concerted effort to correctly match the employee with the job. We must overcome the temptation to place someone if the job available is not the right match. This can be hard for everyone concerned, but it must be done. A poor job match can lead to multiple problems, including an unhappy employer, a dissatisfied client, angry team members, and a stressed job developer. There are some short-cut placement staff who engage in this sort of practice, and it is often referred to as "place and dump." In other words, they make a place-ment, count it in their number of "successes," and then hide from the inevitable consequences. This sort of unprofessional effort does not meet our definition of success and should be avoided at all costs.

There are other significant reasons for ensuring a good job match. We must start with our client and realize that a failed job attempt is very difficult for them. It can make them feel like just one more huge failure in life and dampen their enthusiasm, or even willingness, to try another. It also destroys trust.

The employer with the poorly matched employee is put in the awkward position of having to dismiss a person with a disability, and this can be very unsettling. It is not unusual for that employer to carefully avoid future problems like this by avoiding the pos-sibility altogether.

The family members or other team members begin to wonder if the job developer is really competent.

A very important but often overlooked consequence is that a great deal of money has been wasted in a poorly executed effort.

Job placement can be expensive, and the best way to keep costs to a minimum is to create jobs with a healthy tenure. Everyone profits from this, and it also means that ongoing support time and expenses are reduced. This is realized because as time goes on employers tend to gradually assume more of the support functions, and the employee gets more and more skilled at the job.

It is acknowledged that making the decision on the job match may be a difficult one. With many placements and years of experience it can get much easier, but there is almost always some room for doubt. That is why there needs to be an additional step in the process before the job placement is given a green light. It is yet another reason why the well-executed job placement plan is important.

Let us assume we have a good job goal and we have worked diligently to come up with a prospective job. An employer has offered the job to our client, and we have to give an answer. Unfortunately, the job parameters are somewhat different from those we were seeking. If the client says "yes" and fails in the job, there are serious consequences. If the answer is "no" and we pass on a potentially viable option, we may regret it.

The solution is to advise the employer that we will need a day to provide an answer because we want to make sure we have considered it carefully. Most employers will view this as a prudent move. We discuss the job with our client and provide some time for thought, and we ask permission to review this with other team members. Then, we contact each team member and explain the circumstances, noting advantages and disadvantages. We ask that they say "yes" or "no" to the placement, and collect the results. Typically, this part of the process should not extend for more than a half-day or so while waiting for return calls or whatever. The general rule of thumb is that, if everyone says "yes," it is worth a try. If, in fact, it does not ultimately work out, at least every team member was part of the decision and will share the consequences. Our client makes the final decision, of course, but the presence of team support can be a very big factor in that decision. Likewise, if all the team members are definitely opposed, this can help convince the client it may not be the right job for them. If, however, there is a split decision, it should be deemed a "no." It is almost always unwise to push a job in this kind of situation, and it will often end up a job loss. Worse, there may be sabotage of the placement if key team members are adamantly opposed to it. It is wiser to continue the search for a better job match.

Financial incentives

Financial incentives may sometimes be helpful with an employer who is having a difficult time saying "yes" to a particular hire. When there is a tax credit available for hiring a person with a disability, it can be useful. Sometimes there are some on-the-job training wage reimbursements available through a government agency.

However, many employers prefer to avoid the paperwork and reporting requirements associated with such schemes. A much simpler method for situations like these is a full coverage of the wages for a short trial period. In this scenario, the referring entity retains the client on its payroll and covers all wages, benefits, and insurance coverage. Although this may seem expensive initially, a part-time job at entry-level wages for two weeks is not really that much. In fact, when compared to the cost of the job developer hunting down another job it may be far less expensive. This type of incentive should be used sparingly, but it can be very effective for a reticent employer who has what appears to be an excellent job match otherwise. We must view these arrangements from the long-term perspective to ascertain their true value.

Employment contracts

In the vast majority of cases our client will be directly hired as an employee of the company. This is the preferred arrangement. However, occasionally an employer will be reluctant to have this person on their payroll because of concerns about liability, workers' compensation expenses, or other similar issues. In this situation we can offer an employment contract, similar to a "temp" service or agency. A very brief agreement is best because lengthy, complicated contracts serve as a red flag for employers. It should merely state the basics of the arrangement, clearly and concisely. A sample agreement is shown on the following page.

Notice the simplicity of this kind of agreement. Employers do not like these arrangements to be unnecessarily complicated, and they especially like the fact that they have virtually no exposure to risk whatsoever. It is a hard deal to reject.

The hourly rate to be charged to the employer needs to be negotiated. For many entry-level positions the wage paid to the worker is going to be on the lower end of pay scales. This is just a fact of life and we should all think back to our first entry-level job and the wage it commanded. The wage should usually be commensurate with the rate paid to other workers doing a similar job. An exception to this is discussed later under "sub-minimum wages." Determining the hourly rate to charge the employer should also be simple. Payroll tax percentages and insurance allocations should be available from the organization's payroll department. Here is a suggested formula:

Wage paid	$7.50
Payroll taxes	$0.78
Insurance	$0.37
Administration	$1.90
Hourly charge to the employer	$10.55

Employers realize that if the client were on their payroll they would be paying most of these costs directly themselves. The extra amount levied for administration helps to recover some of the costs associated with processing the payroll. It should also leave a little for the referring organization.

Sample Employment Agreement

1   [Name of client] is an employee of [referring organization].

2   [The referring organization] is responsible for all insurance coverage, including liability and workers' compensation.

3   [Name of client] will perform the following duties at [customer]:

_____

4   The scheduled hours per week will be _____.

5   The customer [the business where the person will be working] will pay _____ per hour, invoiced monthly.

6   [The referring organization] will provide job training and job coaching for approximately _____ hours per week.

7   [The customer] retains the right to cancel this agreement at any time.

_____   _____

_____   _____

_____   _____

(signatures and dates)

Sub-minimum wages

The US Department of Labor has a provision allowing a business or rehabilitation organization to apply for a special certificate for sub-minimum wages to be paid to persons with disabilities. This method is not preferred for individual job placements, but it can be effective in certain special circumstances. For example, if an ideal job is found that matches our client's plan perfectly and would make them very happy on a long-term basis, it might be deemed a worthwhile alternative. This kind of situation usually arises when there is an easily measured output demand and our client is simply not fast enough to keep up with others doing the same work. An example of this might be a factory job assembling a product. There is usually a "norm" established for this kind of work and slow output inevitably means an increase in costs to the employer. (A "norm" is a measured output of work for a defined job based on an average of other, non-disabled workers.) If the decision comes down to having a job based on the individual's measured productivity or not being employed, this may be a method of getting around that obstacle. The requirements for a special certificate are rigorous and require regular documentation of eligibility and productivity. The rules can be found by researching the Department of Labor website (www.dol.gov). (This is usually considered a last resort method.)

Disclosure

The rule of thumb in business is "no surprises." Employers want to know exactly what they are getting into when they hire someone. Obviously, as with all hiring processes, there is certain information related to discriminatory practices that it is illegal to require. Nevertheless, disclosure to the employer of critical facts is a very wise course of action. In the first place, the employer will probably discover this information anyway in time. Depending on what is discovered, it could lead to a serious breach of trust with the referring organization. Second, some kinds of information require disclosure because failure to disclose could constitute negligence. An example of this might be a client who has been arrested for molesting children. A job developer who was aware of this fact and knowingly placed this client in a children's daycare center could be held negligent by a jury if an offense occurred. These records can be subpoenaed by attorneys, and professionals are expected to exercise judgment and refrain from actions which could do great harm. Failing to act when armed with information constitutes negligence.

The solution is really much simpler and safer than withholding information of this type. When the client and his or her support team are developing the plan is the correct time to bring this issue out and discuss it. The truth is that most employers are realistic about matters such as these and know that some of their employees will invariably have issues as part of the deal. They will appreciate being candid about potential problems and will often volunteer to help monitor the client. Truthfulness is the key to success, and hiding critical information is disastrous. If the client or team refuses to consent to disclosure, job development should either be withdrawn or severely limited to certain, safe environments. This is a choice the client needs to make with a process called "informed consent."

Informed consent and client choice

Informed consent is perhaps one of the most widely misunderstood, misused, abused, and distorted concepts in the field of working with people with developmental disabilities. At times it seems like some professionals are given, at most, a 30-second briefing on the subject. This may result in them getting a client's signature on a dotted line and calling it informed consent or client choice. The reality is that it requires a team effort and a skilled, empathetic professional to help ensure that consent is informed and client choices are made within that framework.

We have all heard stories about elderly people being tricked into signing illegitimate contracts for unneeded roofs, overpriced vacuum cleaners, or get-rich-quick schemes. Thousands have lost their life savings because of unscrupulous financial predators. Fortunately, some laws have been enacted which protect persons with limited capacity for making these kinds of decisions but abuse is still rampant.

Persons with developmental disabilities can often be victims as well. The moral dilemma we seem to face too often is either watching a client make a bad choice or being overprotective and making the decision for them. In most situations a well-structured and executed informed consent process can help clients to make healthy choices while preserving their right to make decisions. This is very true when it comes to deciding about a job.

Informed consent means that the client can demonstrate understanding of the decision in question as well as the likely consequences. Signing a document is meaningless if the under-standing of what the signature represents is not present. There is an excellent method of ensuring, to the greatest extent feasible, that informed consent and meaningful choice are present.

First, it requires a fair and accurate representation of what con-sequences are involved. Explaining consequences in words outside the client's range of experience is insufficient. Sometimes it may be necessary to employ visual aids to demonstrate a particular conse-quence. In other situations it may be necessary to use an alternative form of communication, a visit, a trusted adviser, or other means to gain real understanding. In any event, the client must be able to articulate the likely benefits and/or risks involved in the choice being made. When there is doubt if this understanding is present, the support team should try other means of presenting the facts until there is a consensus that the consent to the choice is, in fact, informed. While this may seem cumbersome, the vast majority of choices can be made without taking excessive amounts of time. The right of our client to make these choices is thereby preserved, and dangerous or unhealthy choices can usually be averted.

The truth of this may be demonstrated by carrying an example of such a choice to its logical extreme. If we saw someone who appeared to be blind or had no reading skills about to step off a cliff marked "extreme danger" we would pull them back without hesitation. We would then attempt to get the individual to understand the danger of that choice. No one would accuse us of interfering with their right to choose. In a similar fashion, we can help guide our client away from unhealthy (albeit usually less dangerous) choices using informed consent. It is the same principle using less immediate means.

Another element in informed consent is the right to make less dangerous or unhealthy choices. We all learn (more or less successfully) via this method all of our lives, and the consequences of our past choices help to guide our future ones. Overprotectiveness in the form of denial of consequences deprives a person of these learning opportunities. The question becomes one of balancing the right to choose and thereby learn from natural consequences with the need to pull someone back before they step off the cliff. Our client must be at the center of any such judgment, assisted by trusted family members whenever possible, and guided toward informed consent using a sound process facilitated by a competent professional. There is no guarantee for perfection in this kind of activity, but most of the time very healthy and sound informed decisions are quite achievable.

7

*C*orporate Job Development

In *individual* job development we are searching for a job for a specific individual. In *corporate* job development we are developing a working relationship with a business that we believe will have job opportunities for our clients in general. This is a long-term investment approach because it may take years before any placement actually occurs. Nevertheless, it is a very valuable part of the overall strategy.

Corporate job development targets larger employers offering multiple kinds and levels of jobs. In almost any large company there will invariably be some jobs which are appropriate for our clients. They may not be readily apparent, but they may be found with the cooperation of the employer. This is why it is important to develop a good working relationship with the employer over a period of time. Many times this can happen concurrently with individual job development activities.

All of the strategies discussed previously apply equally well here. We still want to connect with upper management first. This can be far more difficult and time-consuming than with smaller businesses, but it is very possible to do so using intermediaries. Be prepared for months and perhaps even years of slow progress as relationships and trust are established. Familiarity and personal relationships with key staff should be the initial goal, and not a job placement *per se*. It is vital that the organization that is working with the clients maintains a record of credibility and positive image. Large companies will want to look at this kind of information carefully.

One of the best ways of starting to establish a positive working relationship is through involvement with trade associations such as a Chamber of Commerce, business group, or a community service organization. Large companies usually support organizations such as these and have representatives as members. Committee work in these organizations is an excellent method. Over time, it then becomes possible to work out arrangements on a personal level with known parties rather than strangers. Even in large corporations, an amazing amount of business deals are conducted as a result of personal connections. The relationship with the large corporation should be viewed from this perspective. It is a business-to-business situation, but it is facilitated by the personal connection and established trust.

It is true that large employers are usually far more difficult to cultivate, but they also offer advantages that more than make up for this. There is a rule of thumb which sums it up nicely: "easy in, easy out." What this means is that the easier it is to become established with an employer, the easier it is for the employer to end the relationship. The reverse side of this coin also holds true. A long and complicated effort to become established virtually ensures that the relationship will endure for a long time. We can point to example after example of corporate relationships where persons with developmental disabilities have been employed for many years. These kinds of relationships are valuable beyond measure. They tend to endure through economic downturns and market shifts. They provide a sense of security to our clients that make alternatives wither in comparison. The status of being an employee of a large, well-known company imparts a very high level of self-esteem and pride. Over the long run, gross earnings and employee benefits may reach levels otherwise almost unimaginable. One of the best outcomes is that this company can then become a reference for other employers to use in their decision-making. In fact, a successful working relationship with a large company has very often evolved into the company itself taking on the task of selling the concept to other companies. For the job developer, this is as good as it can get. There is nothing we could ever do or say that will carry as much weight with a new employer. This is a long-term investment that pays very handsome dividends indeed.

An interesting phenomenon often occurs when a large employer begins to hire our clients. They report that other (non-disabled) employees express a very positive sense of respect for what their company is doing. It is fairly easy for a company to write a donation check for some charitable cause, but establishing employment for persons with severe disabilities takes more effort. The prevailing view is that the whole idea makes sense to the other employees, and they like seeing these individuals learning to become productive contributors to the "bottom line." There is an innate sense of justice that is piqued as the other employees learn that our clients are far more like them than they are different. They have the same good days and bad days, troubles with relation-ships, stories about vacation trips, and just about every other kind of normal experience. Workplaces are social environments. Little by little, stereotypes are gradually pushed back and replaced with a new-found respect for the person as a person. This is the ultimate achievement in our field, and the pinnacle of integration of persons with developmental disabilities into their own communities.

Job placement with a large employer should begin similarly to job placement with a small employer. It should start with a single, well-screened, well-matched, and well-trained worker. It is critical that this first placement be given the absolute highest probability of success. Although it may sound a little harsh, the first person placed should have the fewest potential conflicts and the most assets we can find. We must accept the fact that this individual will be a pioneer of sorts, and may well open the door for a number of others in the future. Over time, with experience, and with care-fully planned efforts, we can gradually work with individuals with greater challenges as our success becomes established. Patience is a virtue here.

Another variable is added if the large employer has a unionized workforce. This is another whole dimension to the development of relationships, and this work has to be done concurrently as we work with management. Union leaders will have constituents who have family members with developmental disabilities. They can be found through networking, and they may be willing to champion the cause with us. Obviously, this is going to add time and effort to job development but it is still possible to work out good arrangements. It may very well require an addendum to a contract with a special provision for this effort. It would be wise to start, once again, with a single placement and gradually build over time. It might also be helpful to research other unionized employers and study the arrangements that were successful in those situations.

8

*N*atural Supports

The concept of natural supports is widely misunderstood and misapplied. There is a mistaken philosophy that employers should automatically take on large responsibilities (and, ergo, costs) to employ persons with disabilities just because someone else wants them to do so. This view has made the rounds of academia, and even government policies, masquerading as a quick-fix solution to funding shortfalls, inadequate staffing, and inept support service providers. As with many seemingly well-intentioned ideas it begins with a piece of truth but is then distorted beyond recognition. Let us get this concept back on track.

"Natural supports" is the term used to describe how employers can assume responsibility for assisting our clients with issues that surface on the job. It is a very real and extraordinarily valuable outcome that is possible with a well-matched and mature job placement. When there is an attempt to utilize natural supports prematurely or inappropriately there is a good chance that disaster will ensue.

We must first dispense with the notion that employers can, or should be, forced to assume these responsibilities. Whether it is just old-fashioned guilt-mongering or threats of failing to "accommodate" (vis-à-vis the Americans With Disabilities Act), this view is naïve and counterproductive when applied. It originates in the covert belief that businesses are inherently bad and this is a means of forcing them to do something good. It ignores the fact that, first, this premise is basically untrue, and, second, that businesses are smart enough to figure out ways around it if they choose to do so. There are many ways to legally avoid hiring persons with disabilities. They start with the creation of job descriptions containing core requirements so overreaching that there are always rationales to avoid hiring in the first place. Our solution, as described earlier, is to advance the argument that it is a good business decision to hire our clients, and then to demonstrate that this is true.

It all starts with a sound placement process and a good job match. Once again, we employ the long-term investment model here. We invest up front so that, over time, our client gradually becomes more and more familiar with the job, the social environment it brings, and the expectations of the employer and co-workers. Over time, *naturally*, and without coercion of any sort, employers tend to take over some of these responsibilities. This happens because it gets easier and easier to do so, but also because it is a natural evolution of the employment relationship. Our role as this process unfolds is always to be there when needed but less and less so over time. There is no magic formula for how much time is required for this to happen. The operative variables include the supervisor's personality, the number, severity, and frequency of changes in the job, the kinds of challenges our client must confront, and many others. Suffice it to say that natural supports may evolve over months, and sometimes years, and must be allowed to grow at the rate deemed comfortable by the employer (not us!).

The really good news with natural supports is that wonderful dividends can accrue. One enormous benefit is that they increase the range and intimacy of relationships within the workplace. Co-workers will sometimes willingly take on certain tasks, such as training for a new job skill, and in so doing develop a new relationship with our client. Expanded relationships also provide for deeper understanding of social expectations and an enhanced array of role models. (It is true that, on occasion, certain examples of role modeling might make us wince. We have to remind ourselves at these moments that this is the real world and our clients cannot be protected from any and all negative experiences.)

There is another, more self-serving benefit of natural supports. A crude analogy is the image of the entertainer who is attempting to spin a dozen plates on the end of sticks. Starting with one, he gets it going and moves on to another. Then he starts another, but has to return to the first to give it another spin so it does not crash. Then he adds another, and another, until all 12 are spinning nicely. With each, however, he must return again and again eventually to give it another spin to keep it going. This is a lot like what we do with our clients when they are in their jobs. We start with one, and gradually add one after another, but always returning within a certain timeframe to prevent them from crashing. As employers assist us by assuming some of these functions, we are able to place and support more and more of our clients using the same amount of time and resources. Hence we receive a financial benefit as well. In fact, when we are able to nurture these natural supports it becomes possible for one staff person to provide ongoing support to 6, 8, 10, 12, or even more clients without any of them "crashing" with a job loss. This model easily becomes the most cost-effective, efficient, and sustainable method of employing our clients. There is no need for large buildings, inventories, massive capital investment, layers of administration, or excessive insurance costs because of perceived risk. Overhead expense is minimal, direct costs are minimized, and the benefits to our clients are maximized. *Individual job placements, nurtured and allowed to mature gradually with natural supports, are the best overall model of employment.*

The whole issue of supports needs some additional explanation. The definitions of developmental disabilities will vary somewhat, but are based on the premise that support needs will continue indefinitely. This is true with job placements as well, with or without the development of natural supports. Some funding sources arbitrarily attach time limits to the support they will fund. The fact that they do this demonstrates they do not understand the nature or definition of developmental disabilities. Some level of ongoing support should always be planned. Even when everything has been going smoothly for long periods of time, it is still necessary to maintain contact, review performance issues, plan for unanticipated contingencies such as a medical emergency, and keep up with progress. The other concept at work here is career development, which should not end simply because a level of stability has been attained. There will be more discussion on this in Chapter 11.

9

*U*nderstanding the Job

Understanding our clients is the most critical first step. Now we turn our attention to understanding the jobs they might do. When we reach the point where we understand both the client and the job to the point we can predict no significant surprises, we are ready to make a placement. Most of the jobs we will explore will be easier to understand than most of our clients, but it will still take a thorough procedure to reach that point. When we reach that level of understanding about the job, the second "light bulb" goes off. This is the time for the placement.

As mentioned earlier, a tour of the worksite under normal operating conditions is invaluable. It is important to see not only the physical environment, but the social aspects as well. During the tour many questions should be asked of the employer. Rather than being a nuisance, employers tend to view this as a disciplined approach and are encouraged that the support to be provided will use a professional methodology. There is a basic format for analyzing the job in question which mirrors in some ways the placement plan for the client.

Job description

If a job description exists, we should obtain a copy of it. Some entry-level positions, especially with smaller employers, will not have one. In these cases it is even more important to write down the essential functions of the job. It is also important to ask whether there are additional duties from time to time because these might create problems if they are unknown in advance.

Supervisor

It is important to know whom will be directly responsible for supervising our client. It is also important for our client to meet this person. Occasionally a manager will hire a client but then delegate supervisory responsibilities. Success may ultimately depend on the direct supervisor's response to the client hired.

Schedule

Although the work schedule may vary from week to week, the usual hours and days that are expected to be worked should be clearly noted. We should also discuss how and when schedule changes are communicated to employees. A non-reader will need an alternative method of communication.

Technical requirements

The job description may very well specify the technical requirements necessary, but it is also wise to delve into these more deeply. For example, the job description might state "participate in end of month inventory." A technical requirement for this might be reading and writing skills above the level our client could offer. It is best to know and deal with these expectations before the placement is actually made. In many cases an arrangement may be made to provide an alternative method of getting the job done.

Social environment

Since social issues lead to the majority of job losses, this is a critical component. Because of the nature of this component, there will be a great deal of judgment involved. Observation of the people who work at a business and how they interact is the best way to judge how our client will perform in the environment. A good way to ensure a job loss is to rationalize problems our client may have in this area. Nevertheless, when employers are informed in advance of unusual behaviors they will sometimes surprise us by being more than willing to take these on as a challenge. As always, honesty is the best policy here.

Co-worker supports

In some employment situations a co-worker may be asked to handle certain limited tasks. An example might be quality control checks on a given task. While these can be valuable in the right circumstances, it may also lead to real problems if too much reliance is placed on doing this. The co-worker might be sick, on vacation, or working in a different area. The co-worker may also leave the employer and be replaced with someone totally unsuitable for this role. Therefore, co-worker support should be very limited, with natural supports being the preferred model.

Policies and procedures

Almost all employers have established written policies and procedures governing how employees are treated and what expectations exist of them. These should be studied with our client and reviewed in detail. For example, they might state that three unexcused absences are cause for dismissal. We need to make sure our client fully understands these workplace rules at the beginning of employment. Waiting until there is a problem before reviewing the rules is a good way to create problems for all concerned.

Benefits

Wages are typically the first focus of a prospective employee, but benefits are also a significant concern. We should carefully review the benefits offered, such as holiday pay, sick time, health benefits, and others. Sometimes these can turn an ambivalent candidate into an eager candidate. One employee, for example, has remained with a movie theater for years partly because of the free movie passes offered as an employee benefit. In other cases simple misunderstandings about a benefit can cause conflict. For example, a holiday pay benefit may have requirements for working the day before and after the holiday. It is much better to review these well in advance of the event so it is clear what is expected.

Other

This section of the job analysis should capture all of the idiosyncratic aspects of this particular employer and this particular job. What is it that makes it different? Why is it desirable? Or undesirable? Who do we know who has worked here and what did they say about it? What was our reaction to the manager, supervisor, employees? Is this a place we would want to work ourselves? What was the place like physically? Any information of this sort is valuable at this point in the process, and it should be noted as it may come in handy when we report back to our client and the support team.

The entire process of gaining understanding of the job should be done with a view to the future as well as the present. In other words, we need to assess what this job and employer might look like some years from now; working for a placement into a business that is on the verge of insolvency would be a waste of time, for example. Dead-end business sectors are also poor prospects, and some of these may be the most willing to hire because other employees can see the writing on the wall. Employers with perpetual advertisements for the same job should be viewed warily.

There is a very valuable tool at this stage of the process that should not be overlooked. Whenever feasible, the job developer should actually do the job for a period of time first. This can be a very enlightening process that brings out elements in the job otherwise unknowable. After we have done the job ourselves, we are in the best position to train someone else to do it correctly. An employer will invariably appreciate this attention to detail. If we encounter serious difficulties ourselves it will be very hard to train our client. In this event we should conduct a task analysis. A task analysis is simply a step-by-step breakdown of all the elements contained in the task in question. This should be reviewed with the employer and written down as a guide in training. More on this will be found in Chapter 10.

Seasonal or part-time jobs offering less than ideal amounts of scheduled hours should still be considered. These jobs provide the employer with an opportunity to try out the worker, and for the client to try out the job. If we have worked out a good job match, this may very well lead into a long-term job with the desired number of hours. These kinds of jobs also provide a good addition to a resumé and another reference, and they can add to our client's confidence.

One more element to be factored into our job success equation is the possibility of changes in the job duties, workplace, or supervisor. We may not be able to deal with every change that comes along, but we can certainly prepare for the most likely ones. We should at least ask the prospective employer about changes that might be forthcoming, such as the addition of a new piece of equipment or a move to a new location. Change is inevitable, but planned change is more manageable.

At some point, assuming we believe we have a good job match, supported by the client and the support team, we need to close the deal. Good salespeople understand that getting to a certain point is not enough, and that we may just have to ask for the sale in order for it to be achieved. This can be very difficult for some personality types but it is essential that we proceed by asking if our client will be hired. If we have done our preparation work well, the answer will often be "yes."

Now the real work begins.

10

On-the-Job Training

Successful job placements are dependent on a proverbial three-legged stool of components: understanding the client; understanding the job; and on-the-job training. All three are essential. Our method of training is based on many well-known industrial-based systems. We incorporate these systems and simplify them so that training clients while they are doing their jobs will be as effective as possible.

The concept that we are endeavoring to impart here is a new set of skills or a specific kind of knowledge to someone else. It is, in essence, a teaching system equally effective for individuals with learning challenges as for those who do not have these challenges. We employ four fundamental steps, and we retain the ability to modify according to individualized learning capabilities. There will often be a temptation to circumvent the training method to save time, but here again the short-term gain is far outweighed by the long-term benefits. Training should be looked at as a critical investment, and not as an obligatory routine.

Explanation

The first step in the method is *explanation*. This means that we take the time to explain the meaning of what will be done while the job in question is being performed. The explanation must be accomplished using a communication method our client is able to comprehend clearly.

It can be absolutely amazing to realize how many people perform job duties without a real grasp of how what they are doing affects other people or jobs further down the line. It is completely inadequate to recite a list of tasks or procedures without understanding the underlying importance of this. This importance applies to all jobs because otherwise there would not be an employer willing to spend good money to have them done. Often, however, the importance is ignored, disguised, or separated from the cause and effect relationship contained therein. Our job is to analyze the job from this perspective, and to instill a sense of importance worthy of the costs the employer will bear.

Here is an example taken from real experience. A manufacturing customer used to order small plastic bags filled with four bolts, four nuts, and four washers. Several of our clients would count these out, label and seal the bags, and send them back to the customer by the thousands. It was not the most interesting or challenging job by a long shot, but there were a number of severely challenged workers who enjoyed this familiarity and repetition. Staff performed a quality control function in a rather perfunctory fashion. To them, and the workers, it was simply 12 parts in a bag and nothing more. It all changed one day when the customer called and threatened to pull the contract because of quality problems.

As the customer explained it, with justifiable frustration, *his* customer had complained to him and threatened to pull *his* order. Our labor component (packing the bag) was worth about 25 cents. The rest of our customer's order was worth several hundred dollars. In effect, our quality control problem was being leveraged and amplified thousands of times until it was a nightmare for our customer. As it turned out, the small bag of parts was included in a repair kit for large trucks and was sold internationally. When a single bolt or nut was missing, it rendered the kit useless until replacement parts could be obtained. In a recent problem the defective repair kit had turned up in a Saudi Arabian desert hundreds of miles from a distributor and created a lengthy delay for our customer's customer. We were told to either fix the problem once and for all or the contract would be pulled immediately. We fixed it.

Our first step was to meet with our clients and the staff responsible for quality assurance. We gave them a complete explanation of what our role was in this whole process; what had happened in Saudi Arabia; how our customer had been warned; how we had been warned; and what a huge problem we had caused for people thousands of miles away. Prior to this none of them had any idea of how the parts they were packing were used. We then showed them pictures of the finished product in actual use on a vehicle. We pointed out exactly what the bolts and nuts they were packing would actually do when they were finally put to use. We explained what a problem it was for people when the right number of parts was not in the bag we packed for the kit. We also explained the economic impact this had on our customer, his customer, and eventually us as well. We put a picture of the final application up on the wall and reminded people from time to time what role we played in that picture. We also added a second quality control inspection using a digital scale, but we found that we had fixed the problem at the source. Once people had a solid understanding of why their work was important, the problems evaporated. Our clients, as well as our supervisory staff, now understood the role they played.

Clearly, there will be situations where the importance of a job will be more difficult to illustrate. Nevertheless, any job performed incorrectly will inevitably create problems for someone, and if we are able to convey that concept we will be well on the way to success. It may be necessary to employ additional strategies if it appears the understanding is still out of reach. One method is to ask the employer to have a special session with the client explaining the importance of what they will be doing. This can be far more effective than if we only do this ourselves. Another method is to review customer feedback reports, notes to the employer, or any similar source of information related to our client's work. As is invariably the case, we have to individualize these efforts to our specific client to make sure the information is being assimilated correctly.

Demonstration

The second step in the training method is *demonstration*. We need to show how the job should be done using the best of all possible procedures. All jobs need to be analyzed first so that an optimal procedure is established *before* we attempt to train the client to do the job. In many cases we are able to start with the employer's established procedure.

Depending on the size of the employer and the level of detail they employ in job descriptions, we may be able to utilize their procedure as it is. In many, many cases employers have already determined the most efficient and reliable process for completing the job in question. Since we are often dealing with entry-level positions, the employer is probably very experienced in training new employees. In these cases we need to ensure that we are using the precise method that the employer uses. An excellent way of getting the process perfect is to have the employer train the job coach first. This way we can demonstrate proficiency. The worst mistake we can make at this stage is to train the client using an incorrect procedure. It is many times more difficult to change the method, once learned, than it is to train using the correct method the first time. When we have convinced the employer we have it correct, then we can move on to training our client.

Some employers know what they want accomplished but do not have established procedures for making it happen. Here it is very important to actually *do* the job for a period of time to make it as efficient and sustainable as possible, while also ensuring that the quality level is met or exceeded. Quality is far more important than speed here. Speed will come over time, but quality can never be sacrificed.

There are a number of key variables as we work to establish the optimal process for doing the task at hand. These are consistent with principles of "Lean," a system of eliminating waste in any kind of work.

Motion

The amount of motion should be minimized. We should try to imagine looking at a fast-forward video of the job being performed over a period of hours and determine where unnecessary movement is occurring. Locations of supplies or materials should be set where the least amount of motion is required to continue workflow. We may even want to count the number of times we must travel and measure the distance.

Ergonomics

The set-up of the work should minimize bending, stooping, lifting, and other energy-sapping movements. The highest level of productivity is achieved when the work is set up so that a strong workflow may be sustained hour after hour. Jobs set up incorrectly create unnecessary fatigue, and a fatigued worker makes more mistakes and has lower productivity. This is yet another reason why it is good practice to do the job ourselves first, especially when there is a significant physical element. Almost anyone can do a job well for a short time, but continuing to do it incorrectly for hours can take a serious toll. Even when we are dealing with someone who has had a solid history of work, this situation will leave the worker prematurely fatigued. Our reality is that we are often dealing with clients with a very limited work history, and they may take months to develop good work stamina. This process is called "work-hardening," and it is a very real consideration.

Quality assurance

The quality of the work to be done must take precedence over all other factors. Jobs need to be set up so that the process used produces the desired quality of work. This relationship of process to outcome is considered axiomatic in manufacturing and other kinds of work. In other words, *if the correct process is used it will produce the correct outcome.* Conversely, a bad outcome means an incorrect process was used. If, in our training of our client, we end up with a poor outcome we need to look at the process we used to train as well as the process we trained the client to use.

Situational demand

"Situational demand" is a psychological concept that describes a "pull" kind of relationship within a work setting. It basically means that a certain set of variables within a given situation can demand that a worker produce more or better work, or both. There are times when this technique may be helpful with certain employees. Here is an example. Let us imagine a rather slow "bagger" in a supermarket. Left alone, or working in tandem with a slow cashier, we could expect continuing slowness. However, if we matched the slow bagger to a medium-speed cashier, the situation would demand greater speed to keep up. The look from the cashier, the annoyance of customers, the piles of groceries needing to be bagged, all create pressure to get up to speed. No one has to say a word, but productivity jumps. It does not work if there is too great a disparity in expectations because then the situation starts to look hopeless. There needs to be a stretch, but it should be achievable.

Repetition

Benjamin Franklin has been credited with the statement that it takes 21 days to make or break a habit. True or not, we know from experience that it is many times more difficult to change a bad habit than it is to establish a good one. All training should occur with this concept in mind. Great emphasis should be placed on establishing the correct procedure at the outset, and then making it a habit through repetition. Repetition will ingrain the good habit.

Observation

The third step in the training method is *observation*. At this point we need to step back and observe our client performing the task at hand without offering advice or direction of any kind. This is the only way to ensure that the training was effective and that the client has retained it in a usable way.

If there are procedural errors observed, we have to go back to explanation and demonstration for those elements. This needs to happen repetitively until the task is learned completely, retained, and we are able to observe it without offering any assistance whatsoever. This probably sounds more tedious or difficult than it actually is. The clients usually retain most of the job and just need some fine-tuning on a piece of it here and there.

Sampling

Sampling is a statistically proven method of determining whether an entire body of work is consistent with an approved standard by examining a small percentage of it and extrapolating that the sample is representative of the whole. Industry uses this method constantly in thousands of ways. We use it ourselves all the time, although we may not always see it as a system based on statistical probabilities. For example, in a supermarket we may be given a small sample of some product used in a marketing campaign. If we like it, we may buy it because we believe that what we buy will be similar to the sample we tested. Conversely, if we disliked the sample there is virtually no chance we would buy the actual product.

Sampling must begin at a rate of 100 percent. That means that all the initial work must be performed consistent with the established standard for that work without deviation. The amount to be sampled in the future will vary depending on several key variables. Obviously, our experience with the client will make a great difference in how long we need to continue at a given rate. The potential damage to a product or an employer's reputation must also be weighed. The complexity of the job is also significant in making this judgment. When we are satisfied the job is being performed correctly we can begin to reduce the rate of sampling. The rate should be diminished in accordance with the variables just mentioned. Over time, the rate is gradually reduced but never fully eliminated. In other words, even if our client has been doing the job for a year and is performing successfully, we still need to sample a small percentage on a regular basis. It may be reduced to as little as 2–5 percent, but sampling continues indefinitely. This ensures that we know the skill has been retained and there is no compromising of the procedures.

There are several reasons for continuing to sample. First, our clients may simply forget a component of the work after a period of time. This can be especially true for individuals with certain kinds of learning disorders. Second, there may be environmental factors at play such as a new co-worker who has advocated some kind of change or a "short-cut" procedure. There may also be changes in the work itself that create different outcomes while seeming, at first glance, to be the same as when the job was learned. Lastly, sometimes people just get a bit lazy after doing something many times and decide that the job procedures are better circumvented. In any event, attention to the details and continued sampling will catch problems quickly and before a bad habit becomes ingrained.

In some jobs it may be difficult to sample work behaviors because the client will behave differently when they know their work is being observed. An example here would be a relatively independent job where constant supervision is simply impractical. Although it may sound a bit heavy-handed, there are occasions when it is necessary for the job coach to observe surreptitiously. We may want to find a place where we can simply observe our client at work from a distance to make sure that the work is really being done. A classic example of this was a client who just got tired of parking lot clean-up after an hour or two and would find a place to sit and relax. No amount of coaching helped. The only thing that had an effect was the knowledge that, at any given time, the work might be watched. After being caught "sleeping on the job" a few times, the client realized this behavior was not going to be accepted. This kind of sampling and correction was infinitely preferable to the employer getting annoyed and firing the client.

Training tools

Under the "Training Method" umbrella there are many specialized tools to overcome learning disabilities. Tools should be selected on an individualized basis, according to particular learning modalities and needs, and not used in any kind of generic sense. The operating principle is to use the right tool for the right person in the right situation. A number of examples follow.

Graphics

We live in a visual age. A huge amount of our knowledge of the world around us comes in some sort of visual form like television, movies, video games, and the internet. Still, for some unfathomable reason, we often defer to strictly verbal methods while we are endeavoring to impart knowledge to another person. This is even more problematic when we are dealing with people who have cognitive or communication impairments, or both. We unwittingly march on with an onslaught of words regardless of whether or not the meaning is understood clearly. We persevere and then wonder why we were unsuccessful in imparting knowledge. We need to use a lot more graphic and visual aids in our training approaches.

The vast majority of persons with developmental disabilities are either illiterate or have limited skills. Here is an example of how someone with this limitation can learn a set of assignments. A wonderful tool is a set of pictures clearly depicting tasks being performed. These pictures may be arranged on a marker board in the order the tasks should be done. They can also be reproduced on magnetized stock. As the tasks are completed, our client can put a mark beside the respective picture and thereby stay within the correct order. A smaller version of this picture list can be produced and laminated for carrying around in a pocket. The pictures communicate clearly what is to be done and in what order. The marks communicate clearly what has been done and what needs to be done next. The employer or job coach can then see, at any given time, exactly where the task is relative to the overall job list. Our client often finds reassurance in such a list because it removes much of the guesswork and frustration from trying to remember long lists of duties.

Adaptive equipment

Another aid in training is the use of adaptive equipment. This term is used to describe any kind of equipment that makes it easier for our client to perform whatever functions are necessary in the job at hand. There are many kinds of equipment designed specifically for this kind of purpose, but many other kinds of equipment can also be utilized. Here is an example.

Some of our clients, because of cerebral palsy or other physical challenges, may only have functional use of one hand. In the training process, the job coach should place the same limitation on himself and learn to do the job properly from this perspective. This is the only real way to understand the challenge faced by the client, and the best way to come up with workable solutions. Sometimes all that is needed is a way to hold something down while the functional hand does what needs to be done. There are special clamps designed to do this easily and quickly, and they are readily available at industrial-supply companies.

Working from a wheelchair creates a series of challenges for many jobs. Nevertheless, many of these can be overcome with simple modifications or adaptive equipment. The best way to discover what the challenges and solutions are is to actually do the job while in a wheelchair. Workspace table heights can be adjusted, locations of materials can be changed, and physical barriers can be removed. Solving problems should be looked at as an opportunity for creativity and imagination. Some problems, such as fatigue resulting from improperly placed work tools, are much easier to identify using this method.

Over the years the market has responded to needs for adaptive equipment with hundreds of technological aids. These can range from oversized keyboards to exotic robotics. One of the more common applications is a communication device for individuals with speech impairments. All these aids should be viewed from an individualized needs perspective and researched thoroughly before being implemented.

A very important principle to keep in mind is to visualize the job being performed in this new way, rather than only as it has been done in the past. This may be difficult but it works. Once a job has been re-invented in this new paradigm, it serves as an example for others and makes the next transitions much easier.

11

*J*ob Coaching

Job coaching is the service provided to the employee and the employer after the hire and initial training have been completed. It is an ongoing service continuing, in one form or another, indefinitely. The purpose of job coaching is job retention, and if jobs are not retained there is no job success.

There is no simple rule about how much job coaching is necessary in a given situation. This is, once again, a judgment call based on all the variables associated with the individual, the job, the tenure, and so on. There are, however, some good estimates that may be made and these get easier and easier with experience.

The first months

It should be no surprise that the first weeks, and sometimes even months, will typically require the most job-coaching support. This is especially true for someone in his or her first *real* job in a *real* business. This is not intended to offend, but school-based work experiences or sheltered facility jobs are just not the same. In the real world of work our client will usually be surrounded by and interacting with people who are not disabled, and this may be a very new (and scary) kind of experience. We must remember that we all went through something like this on our first job, and it is very natural. The job coach is there to make the transition as smooth as possible. This often means providing a lot of reassurance and emotional support for some time. The role of facilitating communication is also vital. Employer expectations can sometimes be too vague. Family expectations may collide head-on with employer expectations, especially when it comes to old habits like established family activities. There can be some tough decisions during these periods of adjustment, and the job coach needs to work out solutions to problems quickly. There is no substitute for making a good first impression all the way around.

The most critical relationship to establish is with the person who will be the client's direct supervisor. In some cases this is not the same person who did the hiring so there may be some reservations about the new employee right away. The job coach should emphasize his or her role as a problem-solver, and this will create the perspective of value for the supervisor. Potential problems need to be discovered as soon as they arise so they may be resolved without delay. Problems left unattended will tend to fester and grow over time, and these can lead to termination of the employment.

The most important rule of success in almost any arena is "show up." Attendance is vital. Some of our clients do not have this kind of work ethic ingrained in them, but it must be encouraged and supported without exception. Sometimes family members or other support providers have a lackadaisical attitude about attendance and undermine the effort to create the work ethic. This may occur when family or social events are planned without first requesting time off according to established procedures. The job coach needs to jump on these situations and push very hard for maintaining an impeccable attendance record. This is why establishing a trust relationship with other members of the support team early on is so important. Attendance is so critical that it must be emphasized with the client and repeated from time to time.

Different employers, and different kinds of jobs, will lend themselves to job coaching in vastly different ways. Sometimes the presence of the job coach on-site is easy and welcomed. Sometimes it can create issues because of customers or other variables. The job coach needs to be very aware of the comfort level of the employer and react accordingly. The days, times, and locations of a coaching visit need to be set with the approval of the employer and with the intent of minimizing any distractions. Rush hours or other busy times should usually be avoided. In some cases it is just not feasible to be in the exact location where the job is done. Off-site meetings, such as at a coffee shop, can substitute.

Feedback methods

Job coaches should not rely on only one method of eliciting feedback on the client's job performance. Well-timed phone calls to the employer can be a friendly way of seeing how things are going. Casual observations, like coming into the business as an actual customer, provide another perspective. Watching briefly from a distance may add some additional insights. Another good method is asking acquaintances or colleagues to observe when convenient. The more information gathered, from the greatest number of sources, helps to ensure that a true picture is being generated.

One additional information source is an *employer feedback card*. Some employers just find it difficult to come out and say anything negative about one of our clients, but they may make some notes about a problem on a card. The key here is to make it clear, concise, and consume less than a minute of valuable supervisory time. Lengthy surveys tend to be discarded and are useless. The sample on the following page has proven to be very effective in generating new and useful information, and because it is provided on a simple stamped postcard it is actually used. The client's name is omitted on the card but we know who is employed where.

Business _____   Month _____

(Scoring: 1 = unacceptable, 2 = improvement needed,
3 = average, 4 = very good, 5 = excellent)

Attendance   1   2   3   4   5

Productivity   1   2   3   4   5

Interactions with supervisor   1   2   3   4   5

Interactions with co-workers   1   2   3   4   5

Grooming, hygiene   1   2   3   4   5

Other _____   1   2   3   4   5

_____   _____
(supervisor's signature)   (date)

This very simple card contains the most critical performance variables, yet it can easily be completed in 30 to 60 seconds by even the busiest supervisor. As stated above, it will sometimes surface an issue that has been latent but nevertheless requires attention. The cards should be retained in our client's records, and may be used to demonstrate progress over time.

There are several other strong reasons for using these cards. First, they supply a form of documentation that may be useful in negotiating services and funding with funding agencies. Documentation from the employer tends to carry more weight than second-hand reports provided by a job coach. Sometimes additional support and funding is needed, and the cards can be excellent ammunition for that purpose. An additional benefit may emerge when employment is threatened in spite of the fact that performance has been very good up until that time. This sometimes happens, for example, when management changes. A new manager may decide to ignore the fact that our client has been doing very well on the job and, instead, arbitrarily decide to hire someone else for the position. At this point the job coach can request a meeting with the manager and show the good scores on the cards. There is no guarantee this will work, but it has worked in the past because the manager became worried about the grounds for termination of employment after seeing the record documented by the previous manager.

Dealing with minor issues

The job coach needs to embrace a fundamental principle governing the employment experience: *Employers tend to underrepresent minor issues but these will grow over time into major ones.* It is the accumulation of minor issues, leading to employer frustration, which can lead to job loss. It is the proverbial "straw that broke the camel's back" scenario. Minor issues need to be treated as concerns requiring resolution without delay. Attention to detail engenders trust from the employer and prevents frustration from building over time. It is also likely that other concerns exist and are not being reported. Perhaps the greatest argument, however, is that in the event of a major issue we have established trust with the employer that we will work with them to solve the problem. This trust has helped to save numerous jobs over the years in situations where the more likely outcome would have been a job loss.

There is still another significant barrier often present with less experienced job coaches. This barrier is the tendency to rationalize minor issues in the (mistaken) belief that, since they are minor, they do not require attention. This originates from a very normal aspect of human nature—to leave well alone and move on to bigger things. Doing so is wrong for all the reasons detailed above. The job coach needs to treat all issues as worthy of attention. It is especially true that procrastinating about dealing with them ultimately exacerbates problems. The operating principle is *deal with all issues, even minor ones, within one business day.* Employers will respect this level of attention to detail and quick action.

Let us use an example to illustrate this kind of situation. Our client, Joe, has been in his new job for less than a month. The supervisor has already complimented Joe's work on several occasions and seems very happy with the hire. However, she mentions that Joe was 20 minutes late to work this morning. The inexperienced job coach would probably just speak to Joe about it and remind him about the need for punctuality. Instead, she should also politely inquire of the supervisor if this has happened before. We may very well find that it has happened on several occasions and that the tardiness is increasing. We may also hear that Joe has used excuses like a faulty alarm clock or a late bus.

This kind of rationalizing for performance gaps is far too common, usually because it has worked for Joe in more forgiving environments such as school, home, or sheltered employment. If the job coach also succumbs to rationalization, we only compound the problem.

The correct approach is to advise the employer that we will address this problem immediately. The employer may try to assure us it is not a huge concern, but we should emphasize how important it is to meet requirements and not expect special treatment. This is part of the dignity of responsibility.

Our coaching with Joe will always be fact-based, empathetic, and professional. We should avoid creating the perception of sitting in judgment on his behavior, but, rather, point out the rules in the workplace and what these mean in terms of individual effort. Always be fair, but also be firm when necessary. Joe may start out with his excuses for being late and expect that we will accept them. Instead, we need to work each one backward and resolve them all. If indeed an alarm clock is faulty we should help Joe choose a new one that will be reliable. Perhaps we need to see that he buys a second alarm clock so that he has a back-up system. If indeed a bus was late we need to review the schedule to see if an earlier bus is necessary. This should be done, however, with the understanding that buses are often blamed for being late when the real problem was that Joe was late getting to the bus stop. Facts are the goal here, and they will suggest the proper course of action. Fact-based coaching, implemented without delay, needs to be the model.

Team supports

The above example may also further illustrate the need for team-work in resolving these kinds of issues. The vast majority of our clients have other people who are on their support teams and we need them to assist us as we deal with problems. A home provider, for example, is in the best position to resolve issues like getting up early enough in the morning. Sometimes it is a function of just going to bed early enough the night before. The point is that these others are key players in sharing the success of our client and should be included in sharing in the resolution of problems. The clear understanding of this relationship needs to be established at the beginning of the placement process, and not just when a problem arises.

Disciplinary actions

Even the most skilled job coach is not able to resolve all problems successfully without help. Sometimes problems persist in spite of the best efforts. For example, Joe may continue to be tardy. This may be the time to enlist the help of the employer in dealing more firmly with him. We should ask the employer what the policy is relative to this problem, and what they would do with another employee. Usually, a lower-level disciplinary action would be ap-propriate. Many employers feel reluctant to impose a disciplinary action on our clients (until it is too late to save the job) so we need to encourage them to do so. The very act of sitting down with Joe, and giving him a written warning about tardiness, may have a tremendously positive impact on the problem. More serious issues can be addressed with a suspension, which immediately affects the client and still saves the job. Saving the job is, of course, our goal. Over time, the work ethic is gradually established and this type of problem disappears. In fact, once our clients have been in a job for a year or two they often become some of the most reliable employees. It takes some patience and good, effective job coaching but the long-term result is excellent.

Occasionally, despite our best efforts, a client may still sometimes fail to understand or assimilate certain expectations. We may have neglected to account for a well-ingrained problem behavior such as petty stealing, or the client may simply find a particular behavior too rewarding to change. Some issues simply cannot be tolerated by an employer because of strict company policies or liability concerns. An example might be a client who engages in sexual harassment in the workplace. A co-worker who reports behavior of this type must be respected and, in any kind of zero-tolerance environment, the employer is left with no choice but immediate dismissal of the offender.

In these cases we need to offer complete support to the employer while we also offer support to our client in dealing with the job loss. It is critical that our client understands exactly what created this situation and how it can be avoided in the future. This can be a very difficult emotional experience for the job coach, but it can and must be done. It should be viewed as a life experience that, although painful in the short term, will be invaluable in the long term. It is also very important that the natural consequence of being fired is actually a very real consequence that invokes a clear cause and effect relationship between the events. The worst thing we could do is to shield the client from this learning experience altogether. All we would be doing is creating the prerequisites for another, perhaps worse, outcome in the future.

Consequently, we should also avoid helping the client to find another job too soon. As a rule, a week or two of unemployment tends to feel more like a vacation than a real consequence of being dismissed. Therefore, a longer period of time helps to burn the experience into our client's memory. A month, or even a bit longer, usually works just as well as much longer periods to make the point. The real clue that a lesson has been learned is revealed when the client can articulate what happened and why, and what needs to happen in the future to prevent a re-occurrence. If the client continues to rationalize about or deny the problem, more work needs to be done before placement into a new job.

This entire scenario may sound a bit harsh to some, but it has been proven over and over to be the most effective method of instilling long-term healthy work habits and behaviors. Overprotectiveness in these cases will too often cause repetition down the line. Several dismissals for the same reason may end up forming an insurmountable barrier to meaningful employment. We must not interfere with our client's right to learn from their mistakes as we have done ourselves.

Evolution of natural supports

As we discussed earlier, natural supports must be allowed to evolve as the employer gradually assumes more and more of the job-coaching responsibilities. Care must be taken not to force this transition, but rather to allow it to occur over time. There is no magic formula for how long it will take, but it is safe to say that many employers begin to take on additional tasks within a year or two. It may happen earlier when there is already an established working relationship with the employer.

One of the most rewarding moments in a job coach's work occurs when an employer asks to take over some of the coaching duties. This means there is acceptance of our client as a valued employee, that the employment is expected to continue for a long time, and that the amount of time and effort required for this is seen as a good investment. *This is job success.* It does not mean that job coaching ends entirely. Consistent with our principle of sampling work performed, we should continue to elicit feedback at whatever level the employer finds comfortable. With a truly positive working relationship we can count on the employer to call us back for additional assistance whenever needed.

The usual suspects

The "usual suspects" refers to the kinds of issues we are most likely to face, and are therefore the kinds of issues we should be most attentive to while job coaching. There is a problem-solving approach in management called the "80–20" rule. It suggests that 80 percent of problems tend to occur in 20 percent of the possible places, and it is true surprisingly often. It works for us in job coaching equally well.

Earlier on we identified the primary realm of problems resulting in job losses as "social." In other words, in spite of all the potential issues involving technical competence we might face, we deal with social-related issues far more often. These tend to fall into three groups.

The first is *attendance and punctuality*. These are learned social behaviors and part of what we term the "work ethic." Job coaches need to start here and ensure that problems are dealt with swiftly. It is a huge error to assume that a work ethic exists. It must be demonstrated.

The second area is *grooming and hygiene*. We should never assume that appropriate grooming and hygiene will be present. Rather, we should use our own observations and feedback systems to ensure that adequate attention is being paid to these skills. This entire subject area is subjective in nature and is therefore vulnerable to misinterpretation of acceptable standards. Even when no problems have appeared in the past, we should be vigilant because changes in circumstances can cause changes in attention to detail. For example, a new residential services provider may have different attitudes about working with the client on fundamental grooming efforts. Sometimes a personal tragedy, such as the loss of a loved one, may trigger apathy about personal appearance. A new friend or companion may be a less-than-desirable influence. Whatever the reason, we must remain alert for changes with potential negative impacts.

The third area is *relationships with co-workers*. One of the truly rewarding benefits for our clients of working in real jobs is the opportunity to make new friends and establish new relationships. We all do this in our jobs. The reality for many of our clients is that some of these new opportunities may create confusion as to what is or is not acceptable in a given work (read "social") relationship. As a result, our client may misunderstand a friendly gesture and interpret it as an invitation for a romantic relationship. Sometimes the mere fact of working together might suggest that socializing together after work is also desired. In some cases that may be true, of course, but in other cases it is simply a misunderstanding of the social cues. This leads us to a principle of job coaching: *More time and effort will be spent on dealing with social interactions and their potential difficulties than on all other issues combined.* This is the reality, and job coaches need to approach their work from this perspective. Cues and signs of problems need to be discussed openly and quickly, devoid of rationalizations and excuses. Once again, over time, the "dos and don'ts" of the social environment known as the workplace gradually become assimilated and our clients become, finally, accepted for who they are.

When our clients are ultimately accepted the benefits are tremendous. Friendships do become established that extend beyond the workplace and add inestimable value to the quality of life on both sides. Workplace events such as celebrations add yet another dimension to the entire social experience. Many employers go out of their way to make sure our clients are included in these events, and take great satisfaction in knowing they are doing something intrinsically wonderful. The key is to *allow* these kinds of things to occur naturally and at their own pace, and never force them. Pushing these kinds of things on to people who are not receptive creates pushback and resentment, precisely what we do not want.

Career development

Each of us has had career goals we have strived to achieve. Most people have a number of jobs over the course of their careers. Increasingly, dramatic changes in careers are becoming far more likely than staying in one career forever. As our clients develop their skills and add experience to their resumés, we need to view their jobs as steps along a career path as well. There is a tendency to want to see a successful job placement as the "end" rather than the "means." However, the means to a better end is exactly how we should view it.

The first real job we ever had is almost invariably *not* the job we would want to have forever, and this is often true for our clients as well. These first jobs are invaluable learning experiences and sources of references. Nevertheless, they should be seen as a necessary first step to an even more satisfying career experience. Our clients should be coached about the time-tested values most employers hold. For example, short tenures are viewed as "job hopping" and are a red flag for a potential new employer. One- to two-year tenures are usually considered a minimum in this respect. The client should understand about providing adequate notice and completing all duties right through the last day of work.

One of the simplest and best rules is "The Tarzan Principle." It simply means "Hang on to the vine (or job) you have until you have the next one firmly in hand." In other words, do not quit your job until you have a legitimate offer for an even better job. Sometimes, when the topic of a new job is discussed, a client may jump the gun and want to quit immediately. This needs to be thoroughly discussed in advance so that appropriate steps are taken.

The criteria for evaluating a potential new job should be similar to those we all use. These include such things as better pay, better hours or working conditions, greater responsibility, closer proximity to home, better opportunities for advancement, greater independence, and so on. Having the discussion about career advancement may serve as an opportunity to explain the requisites and work them into some goals. This does not mean that career changes are always desirable, but it does mean that we should never assume that the current job should just go on forever. There is no substitute for good professional judgment and timing in this matter.

12

*F*inancial Success

Job success for people with developmental disabilities requires time and effort. The process is an investment that pays long-term dividends for all concerned but requires resources to be expended in its pursuit. There are various structures or models for accomplishing this goal, including for-profit companies, sole proprietorships, volunteer groups, and perhaps others. Non-profit entities organized with the purpose of assisting persons with disabilities are the most common provider of this service. Contrary to a surprisingly widely held belief, non-profit organizations *must* make a profit to survive. It is a very simple equation that governs this reality: *if expenses exceed revenues on a continuing basis the organization will eventually go bankrupt.* Our discussion of financial success will focus on non-profit organizations, although most of the principles will apply in other types of structures as well.

The essential difference between a for-profit and a non-profit organization comes from the statement of purpose or mission statement. For-profit organizations exist to make a profit for the owners or shareholders. Non-profit organizations exist to pursue a charitable mission, and they re-invest their profits in the organization. The two are otherwise, in most respects, similar in basic functions. Non-profit organizations are normally exempt from most (not all) taxes but do incur other unique operating expenses required to maintain their tax-exempt status. Successful non-profit organizations tend to be run in a business-like manner or they usually end up out of existence. This rather stark fact of life seems to come as a shock to many people who are drawn to work in the helping professions. We need to help them get over this delusion.

There are countless examples of well-intentioned but ill-prepared practitioners who have steered their organizations into oblivion by ignoring sound business practices. The missions of their now defunct organizations go unattended and the clients unserved as a result. Financial success ensures that the charitable mission will be served indefinitely, and it is thus a very honorable endeavor.

At times the demise of a non-profit organization may create a sense of theater. Some years ago a director of an organization providing job services to persons with disabilities was given a prestigious state award. The achievement was, in effect, for publicly proclaiming that all the clients served by the organization were to receive much higher wages regardless of their productivity or real earning potential. This director was cheered by a throng of teary-eyed admirers as she went up to receive her award. Just a skeptical few in the audience wondered where all the money needed to pay for this decision would come from. The answer came in about a year when the organization went bankrupt and abruptly ceased to exist. Many of the clients became unemployed overnight, or were transferred to other organizations which then had to begin correcting the problems which caused the bankruptcy. Financial success is not the end, but it is the *means* to the end.

This chapter is not intended to cover a vast array of business methods or principles. Instead, we will focus on several areas most directly related to providing employment services to persons with disabilities. We start with a basic assumption that there is some source of funding dedicated to this purpose. (If there is none, that is an entirely different legal/political subject which will not be pursued here.)

Congress authorized funding for developmental disability services in 1970. It began with funding for institutionalization, and over the years evolved to include community-based services. States administer these funds and there is some flexibility in how they are disbursed. Much of the money is spent purchasing services from non-profit provider organizations. Although some organizations depend entirely on these funds for revenue, financial success is far more likely when other sources are also utilized. This is far easier said than done. We will return to this subject after a description of the various kinds of service models.

Over the last 60 years or so the models of service delivery have evolved from horrific institutions right out of the middle ages to a broad range of mostly community-based systems and structures. The range of quality to be found is equally broad. Some are shining stars of excellence with innovative, respected, and first-class operations in all aspects. Some still resemble the middle-age institutions we would like to think we have left far behind. Many are just testimonials to mediocrity that have still managed to gain some acceptance and tolerance. A discussion of the quality of organizations is similar to a discussion of the quality of doctors, or lawyers, or any other profession. If you have seen one organization, you have seen just one organization. Generalizations based on a simple description of a model of service are simply not adequate. Nevertheless, we will describe some models because they are all still in use and they all have relevance in a discussion on financial success.

- *Work-activity programs* (or day programs, alternatives to employment, community inclusion, and so on) were some of the first services located outside of institutions. Groups of persons with disabilities engage in a variety of activities intended to contribute to the clients' quality of life.

- *Sheltered employment facilities*, often called "workshops," became common in the 1960s and 1970s. The vast majority of the employees are persons with disabilities and their products are sold to businesses or government agencies.

- *Work crews* (such as a janitorial crew) take on contracted assignments in community locations under the supervision of a staff person.

- *Enclaves* are groups of workers with disabilities (usually no more than eight) located within a larger business, with a supervisor employed by the provider organization.

- *Affirmative businesses* are businesses operated similar to a for-profit business under the auspices of a non-profit organization. Many, but usually not more than half, of the employees have disabilities.

- *Self-employment* refers to a business owned and operated by a person with a disability.

- *Individual job placements* are jobs where one or two individuals with a disability are employed in a for-profit business or government agency and receive job-coaching services to help maintain their employment.

There has been a tendency in the past to view these models as a kind of hierarchy through which clients routinely moved on to greater and greater levels of independence. Sometimes this passage was even looked at as a kind of graduation rite. The problem with this perspective was that many of the clients, if not most, did not move on. Rather, organizational inertia took hold and people often stayed where they were indefinitely. Sometimes the underlying, but often unnamed, reason for this was a financial disincentive against moving. When an organization is heavily invested in a particular model it can be very expensive to change.

We are focused on individual job placements because of all the benefits we have described earlier. Overcoming organizational inertia requires that we show that not only is this the best model for employment, it is also the most cost-effective. We do so with an acknowledgment that not everyone is appropriate for any given model, and all services should be individualized to meet a specific individual's needs. Nevertheless, far more persons with developmental disabilities have the potential to have fulfilling careers in the real world if only we remove more barriers from this dream. The first barrier to attack is transitioning to the individual placement model while remaining financially healthy. Financial success can be achieved by using the following management methods.

Minimize overhead expenses

All of the facility-based models described above require significant amounts of capital invested in buildings. Some organizations have spent many millions of dollars on these facilities and are emotionally, as well as financially, attached to them. This contributes to the organizational inertia even more. A good place to start on this journey is an objective assessment of the true costs of maintaining a facility. It is simply inaccurate to only weigh the costs of developing individual job placements against a facility-based operation without this kind of analysis.

For this example let us assume the organization has a building worth US $1,000,000. If it is financed there will be a mortgage payment. If it is leased it will be even more expensive because the building owner will have to realize a profit. There will be significant amounts required for insurance (fire, business loss, property, property of others, liability, workers' compensation, and others). Maintenance and repairs can be very costly. A reasonable amount must be set aside annually for replacement through a depreciation amortization schedule. Utilities, cleaning services, furnishings, security: the list goes on and on. Thus far, all of these costs have not produced one minute of service for one person with a disability. Worse, the costs continue regardless of the level of income being generated. In difficult economic times they can serve as an anchor pulling the organization into insolvency. Overhead expense, therefore, is the enemy of financial success and quality services.

One more calculation needs to be made in the case where a facility is fully paid off. Even when there is no mortgage or debt whatsoever, the true cost must be determined by analyzing the return on investment realized. Using the building above as the example, if it were sold and the funds invested at even a 4 percent rate of return, $40,000 annually could be realized with minimal risk or effort. That is in contrast to all of the expenses listed. If this calculation is not included, it is not possible to have a true picture of the cost savings.

From a purely financial perspective, one of the great advantages of the individual placement model is the low overhead expense it requires. In this model, the staff need only a part-time office, a cell phone, and a car to do their job effectively. The prospect of changing from a facility-based model may be daunting because it is really not feasible to do this overnight. In fact, some type of smaller facility is almost always needed as a back-up when serious problems emerge. In addition, making the transition can require several years and both kinds of services need to be paid for simultaneously during this time. Once again, this kind of goal requires long-term thinking so that a bridge of funding may be allocated to the purpose. In larger organizations with multiple facilities it is actually much easier to accomplish since transition can occur in measured steps. Minimizing overhead expenses will pay dividends financially as well as for the quality of services, because the savings may then be utilized for more and better services.

Minimize administrative expenses

There are other kinds of overhead expenses which also require attention so that they may be kept at a minimum. Administration is the most obvious here. Top-heavy organizations with excessive levels of bureaucracy are still common. Modern management practices shun these and replace them with streamlined, lean, "flat" structures having few levels of authority. The "old-school thinking" that created these organizational dinosaurs is still around and defended by many of its beneficiaries, but they are doomed to die a slow death in the coming years. "Lean"-managed organizations will survive and thrive in the future because they are committed to eliminating waste of all kinds. This concept has its own body of literature so we will focus on just a few of the basics here.

A flat organizational structure means that a chart of the positions, ranging from CEO to staff on the front-line, would have a relatively flat appearance. There are minimal levels in the hierarchy, usually only two to four depending on the size of the organization. Compare this with a government agency where there may be 10, 15, or 20 levels of authority. Not only is this extremely wasteful and expensive, it makes the overall functioning slow, inflexible, and unresponsive to changing conditions. Some non-profit organizations mistakenly emulate government agencies in how they are structured and function. The correct model, using our own mission instead, is a successful lean business using the mission as the driving force.

All management models have advantages and disadvantages, but lean administration is essential for financial success. Administrative staff are management, accounting, clerical, public relations, and other staff who do not provide direct services to clients. There are differing views as to what an acceptable level of spend on administration is, but we will submit that 12 percent of the total operating budget should be a maximum amount. Several years ago a new service brokerage agency was created with a 33 percent administration budget (100 percent funded with taxes), and the creators defended it unabashedly. As expected, it is heavily bureaucratic and woefully inefficient. If it were financed with anything other than tax-payer's money it would be out of business already. Few non-profit organizations can operate like this for very long.

Accurate financial reporting

Regardless of the size of the organization, fast and accurate financial reporting is critical. Simplicity and clarity should be the standards for reports, and performance should be known within two weeks of the close of business in any given month. Financial reports are a form of statistical process control, and they point management into the areas that need attention. The longer a problem continues unattended, the greater the severity of its ultimate impact. There are cost-effective accounting tools available for organizations of any size, and these should be a part of their foundations.

A key part of the financial report is a realistic budget. Actual performance needs to be compared with budget figures so that variances from budget are clear. This is a fundamental management tool and keeps operations from straying too far from the target. As simple and seemingly obvious as this would appear, many struggling organizations failed to adhere to these basics. An honorable mission is no substitute for common sense and business "savvy."

The financial reporting system should be in a business format rather than a government agency format. A business format has a section for sales, cost of sales, and margin on sales. Lacking these it is impossible to tell whether any money is being made on revenue-generating activities such as a labor provision contract. Government agency reports usually use a "fund accounting" method which does not provide for sales, and they typically are not clear or simple to understand. It is one of the reasons government agencies so often have funding crises or spending splurges.

Creating the budget is part of achieving financial success. Starting from scratch is always based on estimates, but once operational it is possible to achieve a very high degree of accuracy in forecasting. Expenses should be budgeted liberally, and revenues should be budgeted conservatively. There are four basic components for every line item of revenue or expense.

- *Actual*: this is what has really happened over the last 6–12 months. The amount can be entered into a very simple spreadsheet and averaged into a monthly amount for comparison purposes.

- *Budget*: this is the projected amount, stated always in the same unit of time, usually per month.

- *Variance*: this is the difference in dollars per month between "actual" and "budget" for the particular line item that is being projected. Significant differences need to be explained and corrective action taken.

- *Variance percentage*: this is the same as above but restated as a percentage of change from budget. This figure helps us to look at the budget from a different perspective, and it puts simple data-entry errors into the spotlight for correction.

This entire spreadsheet format is extremely simple and, after a couple of years, may be completed in very little time. Existing budgets can be saved and easily updated, which eliminates repetitive data entry. After a little practice they can be completed in under an hour and are extremely accurate.

Maximize revenue

This section is really a bit more than the cliché would suggest. There is often a tendency to shoot for one big windfall event, but it is the continuous improvement in small increments over time that produces sustained success. Each operational function needs to be analyzed for ways to generate additional revenue. How this is done depends on what sources are present, of course, but we will look at a few likely examples.

If services are provided on a "billable-hour" basis, the work schedule is a key variable. It often helps to start with an "inside-out" approach, with the middle part of the day scheduled first and the early and late parts of the day scheduled later. This helps to eliminate holes in the middle of a daily schedule that cannot be billed. In a billable-hours environment, downtime (or, hours that are not billed) should not exceed 20–30 percent of all work time. This can be difficult to achieve but it is essential for getting as much out of each day as is feasible. Other non-billable tasks, such as meetings, travel, training, and similar things, should be kept within that percentage. These activities may be necessary but they are not considered value-added work for our clients and should be kept to a reasonable minimum. A percentage of billable hours versus non-billable hours should be calculated periodically to stay on track.

The same principle may be applied in an arrangement where there is a set fee for ongoing support. In this case the amount of time spent on direct services should also be calculated in the same way as billable hours. This way the value-added time can be maximized allowing for additional clients to be served for the same staff expense. This also maximizes revenue.

Another way of providing employment is through the use of an employment contract. Sometimes employers prefer this arrangement to having the worker on their payroll. In this situation it is important to carefully calculate all the indirect costs of labor (insurance, Social Security, unemployment taxes, and so on) and then add an administrative amount on top. This should be a relatively small amount (in the 6–10 percent range), but it helps cover additional expenses and is ultimately another source of revenue. Employers typically find this charge very reasonable.

Grants are another potential source of revenue but these should be viewed with some caution. First, most foundations offering grants require that the money is not used as a substitute for existing revenues. Second, they tend to avoid funding normal operating expenses and, instead, prefer to fund "projects." One way to utilize these funds for a project is in the form of building capacity, starting a new service, or expanding geographically. They should definitely be used for things like office space or a needed building. This way all other operating revenues may be used to provide services rather than funding a physical plant.

Donations are another source of income to be developed over time. However, it is easy to spend more time and money chasing after donations than the sum that is ultimately received. The best method is to cultivate positive relationships with businesses and individuals who believe in what you are doing. As they see the results and receive information (such as a newsletter) about successes there will be people who want to support what is going on.

An excellent method is to have another entity, such as a service club, conduct a fund-raising campaign on your behalf.

Donations and grants should usually not be included in budgets unless a particular grant requires it. This way, revenues are not committed and any extra funds received can be placed into reserves.

Establish reserves

Reserves are simply funds that can *and should* be saved. Any unusual or unexpected revenues that come in should be ignored and placed into a special reserve fund. All businesses need a reserve fund with a minimum of three months' operating expense in it. This can take time to establish but it is essential to handle unexpected problems or economic downturns. The three-month reserve level should be the minimum, and there really is no maximum. Successful operations generate goodwill from employers, businesses, community members, families, and others who will want to see our clients served well into the future. Donations will come, sometimes in the form of a beneficiary from an estate. It is perfectly acceptable to acknowledge this kind of option to those who might be so inclined. Eventually, the reserve fund can become an endowment fund and create a healthy financial future indefinitely.

Diversify

Most successful businesses learn that diversification is extremely important. This does not mean that the mission should be changed. It does mean that funding sources should be as varied as possible. Typically, whenever more than 20 percent of all revenues come from a single source this a cause for concern. Diversification helps to shield the impact of unanticipated budget cuts or other financial dilemmas.

Diversification also applies when it comes to placing our clients with employers. Although it may be tempting to place more and more clients as employees of a given company, restraint is the wiser path. The 20 percent rule applies equally well here. If there were too much dependence on one employer a catastrophe could result if that business were to fail.

In summary, financial success is not just a desirable goal—it is absolutely essential if we are to be able to provide quality services for our clients. The basic principles are direct from business management and modified only slightly to fit our operations. Financial success is not the *end*—it is, however, an essential *means* to the end of job success for our clients. This relationship should be understood and articulated whenever necessary.

13

*H*iring and Training Staff

The quality of an organization, and its services, is exactly equal to the quality of its staff. The most important management function is the hiring, training, and supervision of staff. Providing services to people with developmental disabilities is a specialized niche with specialized duties. Although there are college degree programs which incorporate elements of these specialized duties, few if any provide a focused preparation for securing employment opportunities for our clients.

The emphasis on financial success outlined in the previous chapter provides a starting place with regard to hiring staff. Despite all the rewards associated with assisting persons with disabilities, employees still need to make a good living. This demands the resources necessary to pay competitive wages, provide good benefits, and offer as much job security as is feasible. Failure to do so will mean that the best employees will simply not be available for hire. At times it has been astounding to note that some organizations (or funding agencies) operate with the mistaken belief that high-quality staff will somehow magically appear even when the compensation is at the lowest end of the scale. The truth is that excellent staff demand competitive compensation. In the long term, great staff generate more revenue and provide the quality of service that generates more business, so it is yet another investment. There is an old saying: "Do things right, and money will follow." It is very true with staff.

In much the same way that we approached the cost of employee turnover in our discussion about employers, we deal with the exact same issue in our own employment efforts. The cost of recruiting, hiring, and training a new competent staff person can easily exceed the value of four to six months of wages. Unnecessary turnover, in effect, is waste and needs to be avoided. There are many, many problems generated by excess turnover. These include loss of experience, employer dissatisfaction, client issues that result in job losses, loss of trust with family members, loss of supervisory time for quality assurance, missed opportunities, and many more. Quality staff with good tenure is the key to success in all areas.

The myth about staff

First off, let us deal with a pervasive myth that seems to come up far more often than we would ever expect. This myth is that almost anyone can secure employment for persons with developmental disabilities. Whenever something very difficult is done extremely well, like playing a violin or making a three-pointer in basketball, the highly skilled and trained virtuoso does tend to make it look much easier than it is. This holds true in our field as well. Outside observers who have never attempted anything similar take a glance and somehow think they can also do the job. Time and time again we have had to come in and fix the damage done. The damage is real, and sometimes it is long-lasting. An employer burned by an inappropriate job placement has been known to avoid hiring persons with disabilities for many years. A client who was placed in a poorly matched job has been known to refuse any other job opportunities. These are not isolated incidents. They are just a sampling of the havoc wreaked by unskilled practitioners.

The right combination

For our purpose, the best staff do not fit easily into a category. They do not necessarily come from a certain college background. They do not necessarily have experience in this particular kind of work, much less experience in the field in general. In fact, it is usually preferred if they do not have any direct experience in the work. This is because they often come with the wrong philosophy and bad habits. There are, however, some general kinds of transferable skills from other occupations that are very helpful. When combined with the correct attitude we have the makings of a great staff person.

Some skills seem to show up on lists of attributes on virtually every resumé. These include great teamwork, communication, and other more generic skill sets. The reality is that many people are not particularly good at communication but almost always believe they are. Effective communication with persons with developmental disabilities is a deal-breaking kind of skill. It has to be there and it has to be excellent or the person will simply be unable to function effectively. It is not good enough for a candidate to note a certain number of years of experience in the field, or a relevant degree, or whatever. In fact, some of the worst communicators ever encountered have had years of experience working with people with disabilities.

Excellent communication skills are a combination of intelligence, self-awareness, empathy, focused training, and responsible experience. These skills must be based on a consistent approach of treating persons with disabilities as equals. An employment interview can give good insights into this area but may not be sufficient alone. One additional technique is the inclusion of a client on the interview team. Providing this person with some interview questions and letting nature take its course can provide an excellent measure of how the candidate interacts with the client. It is not intended to be a complete measure but it does help to give a broader perspective. The client's perspective can be very helpful in weeding out people who make them uncomfortable.

Communication skills with clients are essential, but supporting a person in a job requires the ability to communicate with employers as well. This means that the candidate must have the ability to understand an employer's perspective. Businesses face financial pressures on a daily basis, and the performance of their employees is a critical component in their ability to meet these pressures successfully. Staff candidates who only have social service backgrounds often (although not always) struggle to gain this awareness. Despite this, the prevailing wisdom seems to be that social services is the best place to look for candidates. We disagree.

The best staff hires have been candidates with good business experience. If they have excellent communication skills they quickly learn to communicate well with our clients. There also seems to be an intuitive positive response to our clients' efforts to become productively employed. What has usually been a dismal failure has been the attempt to teach business concepts to new staff having only social service experience. They almost invariably struggle to relate to employer concerns with the necessary degree of insight.

The crème de la crème come from the ranks of actual employers of our clients. The first-hand experience gained from previously working with our clients (often as front-line supervisors or department managers) empowers them in a way that is unmatchable. They already know what can be achieved. They are already believers in our mission. They already have positive working relationships with our clients. They can speak to employers as peer-to-peer in a way that overcomes barriers with ease. They understand the trials employers face and they can offer testimonials of how our clients can be valuable to them. Added benefits are the established networking and business contacts they bring with them. It is far easier for them to gain an audience with a prospective employer.

The problem is that it takes time and a lot of hard work to get to the point where such a person is willing to take the risk of making this kind of career change. It can, and does, happen but the organization must have a reputation for integrity, quality, and financial wherewithal to be seen as a worthy employer. This is yet another example of the value of investing in long-term financial results.

There are innumerable training aids available which cover generic hiring principles. These can be great resources. Our efforts incorporate these, of course, but focus on the very limited range of best candidates for a highly specialized kind of job. While there are certainly some experienced candidates available, they often retain some undesirable attitudes or philosophies. One of the most dangerous attitudes is the approach in which job placements are made without detailed attention to appropriate matching. This sloppy method has been far too common and has created even more barriers to overcome in the long term. Care must be taken to avoid hiring staff with this kind of experience.

There are a few other problem types of candidates to avoid at all costs. One is the "protective mother" type who wants to nurture and protect our clients from anything and everything. This kind of person comes in both sexes and will create a dependency relationship that is very harmful to clients. Another is the person who believes they are on some sort of heavenly ordained mission, and may try to convert our clients to their religion or otherwise "save" them. Yet another is the overly liberal social worker type with an axe to grind against the "evils of business." They all exist, and they will all lead to disastrous results.

Training

One of the perils inherent in hiring a new staff person is the immediate need to have someone doing the work in spite of the fact that there has not been sufficient time for thorough training. This is a trap that must be avoided. Despite the hardship, we should always invest in proper training before sending a new member of staff out into the world. The "sink or swim" method produces a lot more sinking than swimming. At a minimum, three or four weeks should be devoted to training before working alone. Within a week or two the new person may be accompanying the best staff on visits to businesses and clients. Watching an experienced professional is an essential tool in the training process. Debriefing after visits, complete with questions about observations made, is part of this effort. Attention should be paid to why certain things were said or done, and not just the actions themselves. In time, toward the end of the training period, some trial runs may be scheduled with some of the safer, more established employment sites.

The other part of the training is more academic. The training method detailed earlier for clients should also be used with staff. (*Explain, Demonstrate, Observe, Sample.*) The focus should start with the mission and how it is realized through the work the new person will be doing. A training checklist should be utilized, which details the items to be covered and documents the time spent, the date, and the trainer. It is very effective to use a number of professionals for this purpose as the trainee will become desensitized working with only one person hour after hour. A good model is one- to two-hour segments with changes of instructors each time. This is why the checklist is so important. A sample checklist is shown on the next page.

There have been two main approaches to structuring the duties required in our field. The first is to have separate job descriptions and staff for the functions of *job developer* and *job coach*. This evolved because job development typically requires much more of a sales aptitude than does job coaching. At first glance this approach does appear to make sense. However, experience has shown that this creates more problems than it solves. Because we define job success as sustained employment, the bulk of the work tends to fall into job retention. This necessitates a level of investment on the part of the staff to match jobs and clients far more carefully. When there is a separate job developer this kind of investment is far less likely. In fact, there is a tendency to come up with a job opening and say "there you go!" as if the real work was now over. That, as we have seen, is simply not the case.

The most effective model is a combination of job developer and job coach called *"Employment Specialist."* The employment

Staff _____	Date _____	
Training item	**Time**	**Instructor**
1 Mission and philosophy		
2 Communication guidelines		
3 Organizational structure		
4 Payroll and work schedules		
5 Relationships with families, funding		
6 Relationships with businesses		
7 Policies and procedures		
8 Job-placement procedure and philosophy		
9 Job-coaching procedures and philosophy		
10 The training method		
11 Records of service delivery		
12 Client records		

specialist handles all of the responsibilities of both positions and is evaluated on long-term results (sustained employment) rather than short-term results such as job offers alone. This arrangement also eliminates friction between staff, which may occur when a job has not been investigated thoroughly enough, or when a job loss occurs and the job developer blames the job coach. It also provides a greater variety of duties and ultimately makes for greater job satisfaction.

The best reward for an employment specialist is being able to watch the transforming experience a great new job can create for one of our clients. This reward seldom comes quickly, and this point should be emphasized to a new staff person. Deferred gratification may be difficult, but when that first successful job placement is engineered the result is tremendous satisfaction and the motivation to start on another. This, in fact, is what keeps people in this work for many years. Poor compensation can be justification for not entering the field, but successful job placements are the reason for staying there. There are few comparable rewards in any profession. One of the most gratifying experiences is patronizing a business where one of our clients is employed and seeing him or her working successfully right alongside everyone else, totally accepted, and realizing their full potential as a member of society.

The nature of the job of employment specialist is such that independent work and judgment is essential. Employment specialists need to be empowered to deal immediately with the vast majority of issues they will encounter. Direct supervision is simply not feasible for most of the time. Nevertheless, quality and consistency need to be assured so more indirect methods of supervision are required. It is good practice occasionally to follow staff to observe their work and provide feedback. This can only be done on a very limited basis, however, so there are several other effective methods of providing supervision.

The first of these is a weekly staff meeting to review individual clients and their jobs. The meeting should be structured and purposeful with a focus on identifying potential problems as early as possible. When these issues are presented it should serve as a "brainstorming" session aimed at resolving problems while they are still small. Creativity is encouraged when everyone participates in coming up with new and better ideas. This also helps to establish the continuity of quality from one staff member to another. The focus should be forward, looking at dodging potential problems in the future, rather than looking backward at past mistakes. Early warning signs are most easily detected in this manner and solutions may be devised.

All meetings should have an agenda. The notes from the previous meeting should form the basis of the agenda. The notes should consist of brief action plans with assigned responsibilities and dates for completion. They should not be a wordy diary of general events. As each action item is reviewed it may be assessed for effectiveness. When all the action items have been reviewed, new issues are discussed, and action notes are taken. There are three main results of this method. First, accountability for taking needed actions is established. Second, these important items are recorded so they are not lost or forgotten. Third, it is an excellent method of providing indirect supervision and quality assurance.

Another method of ensuring quality is to periodically reassign staff to work with different clients. This provides several main benefits. First, it helps to prevent "burnout" from working with the same person for too long. Even great staff sometimes fall into a routine and may start to miss seeing details. A new set of eyes on a situation sometimes provides fresh new insights. Second, it helps to prevent the client from becoming overly dependent on the staff person. Changes are part of life, and these occasional changes help the client to learn to make these adjustments without too much trauma. The fact that the original staff person is still around is also reassuring. Third, it helps prepare for coverage when a staff person is ill or on vacation. Last, staff should be changed if the supervisor suspects that the employment specialist has become too emotionally involved with the client. Professional objectivity is sacrificed when this situation occurs. The technique should not be overused, but a change in employment specialists every few years is generally a healthy practice.

The work of an employment specialist can be extremely rewarding, but it may also be emotionally taxing. This is especially true if there is a job loss. Even when excellent work has been done, sometimes things happen that are just not predictable. Sometimes an employer has to lay off workers. Sometimes a client does something completely unexpected and is fired. Sometimes outside events, such as a dramatic change in a living environment, may cause job loss. Occasionally a medical condition makes it impossible for the client to continue. When there is such an intimate working relationship a job loss can be very hard on the employment specialist as well as the client. The support of the team is very important at these times.

We have already defined job success. Now let us turn to defining a successful jobs program. We know that there will always be some unavoidable job losses. Nevertheless, when we take care to understand our client, and the job, and we engineer a good job match, we are able to realize a high percentage of successful placements. Experience has demonstrated that following these procedures can and does result in a success rate approaching 90 percent. In other words, after six months the client is still employed, likes the job, and the employer is happy with the client as an employee. Lower rates of success indicate that short-cuts were taken or full understanding was not achieved. If a big surprise is experienced after placement, it means one or both of our "light bulbs" never really went on. Good procedure produces good outcomes.

It is also very important to celebrate successes. A great new job opportunity is a perfect excuse to get together and have a celebration. Meeting a goal or overcoming a major obstacle are also great reasons. The success of the clients and the success of our staff are a direct result of effective teamwork, and the supervisor should reward it.

A sample job description for an employment specialist is shown on the next page.

Job Description

Position: Employment Specialist.

Purpose: Assist clients with developmental disabilities in securing employment, retaining employment, and achieving their full potential in the career of their choice.

Supervisor: Team leader (or manager or director—the titles vary).

Qualifications: Responsible experience in business or rehabilitation; excellent oral and written communication skills; ability to relate positively to persons with disabilities; computer proficiency; valid driver's license with good record; pass criminal history check required; customer service experience; bachelor's degree in business administration, psychology, or relevant field preferred.

Salary: Negotiable depending on qualifications.

Hours of employment: Monday through Friday with occasional evening or weekend work required. Full-time but will vary occasionally.

Working conditions: Office and wide variety of businesses and employment sites in the community, indoors and outdoors.

Physical requirements: Standing, sitting, driving, occasional lifting up to 30 lb.

Responsibilities

1 Develop positive working relationships with employers through business groups, public relations activities, and networking.

2 Develop understanding of client skills, interests, and challenges.

3 Seek out and develop job opportunities using prescribed procedures.

4 Conduct task analyses of potential jobs.

5 Match clients with appropriate job openings.

6 Provide onsite training and ongoing support to clients when employed.

7 Provide technical assistance to employers for working with clients.

8 Provide counseling to clients on overcoming problems which may interfere with their ability to be employed.

9 Develop positive working relationships with family members and other service providers to help the client remain employed.

10 Document services delivered and maintain accurate case records.

11 Drive to and work in a variety of employment settings.

12 Participate in weekly staff meetings.

13 Other related duties as assigned.

14

*M*ythology

There are a number of myths about employment for persons with developmental disabilities. They originate in a variety of places and tend to stake out the extremes of perspectives. Sometimes the source is an ideology based on wishful thinking rather than pragmatic experience. In other cases the source is an ivory tower view from the desk of a government office. Society at large often succumbs to outdated stereotypes or preconceptions. Policies and policy-makers too often embrace these without using real-world practitioners as guides. We will attempt to refute some of these myths using the value of direct experience.

Myth 1: Persons with developmental disabilities are not capable of productive employment in real businesses

Our previous discussions have all been based on real employment situations and real successes. The stereotype of our clients being unable to work productively is an unfortunate product of a history in which people with severe disabilities were not provided with opportunities to work. It thus became a kind of self-fulfilling prophecy. The fact is that, given appropriate preparation, training, support, and opportunities, many if not most people with developmental disabilities *are* capable of working productively in jobs in the community. They typically want to be like anyone else—productive, self-sufficient, independent, tax-paying members of society. More often than not the most significant barriers they encounter are artificial ones created or encouraged by others, rather than their disabilities *per se*. If the people around them do not believe it is possible for them to work, it creates a negative expectation, lowered self-esteem, inadequate preparation, lack of real-life learning experiences, and emotional duress. Positive expectations tend to produce positive results.

Myth 2: All persons with developmental disabilities can hold down an individual job

This is the opposite extreme of Myth 1. It tends to come from overzealous advocates or government employees who seem to believe that wanting something to be true is enough to make it come true. Unfortunately, not all persons with developmental disabilities have the capabilities of being employed in individual jobs. Sometimes the manifestations of the disability are just too severe for employers. There are some issues, like uncontrolled incontinence, sexual harassment, or violence, that employers just will not tolerate regardless of the level of support provided. Fortunately, these kinds of severe barriers affect only a small minority of individuals in our discussion. Our clients are like everyone else in that they experience the same kinds of problems as everyone else.

The fact is, as stated above, many, many persons with developmental disabilities have the potential to hold down an individual job given the right kinds of opportunities. Moreover, many of the rest have the potential for other kinds of employment such as an enclave, work crew, affirmative business, or self-employment. Sheltered-facility employment may still be an option until these opportunities are available, but it should be as time-limited as possible to avoid inertia taking hold.

There will be some clients who, for a variety of reasons, will decide that employment does not add to the quality of their life. We should make sure that opportunities are always available, but we should respect their choice if it is truly informed and not imposed.

Myth 3: Once a person with developmental disabilities is placed in a job, the support work (and funding) is over

This is simply untrue. As we have seen, one of the cornerstones of job success is ongoing job coaching. Problems inevitably arise, and a good job coach helps to guide both the employee and employer to a solution. Circumstances change, and these changes may sometimes be very difficult to assimilate without a helping hand. The modern workforce must be able to change quickly and adapt to new conditions. Even something as common as inclement weather can create confusion and conflict.

Over time, as experience accumulates and natural supports grow, the amount of job-coaching support can gradually diminish. It should never disappear, however. Some level of funding should be kept in place indefinitely so that unforeseen events can be managed and eligibility for support services maintained.

A directly related concept is that service requirements (and the need for funding) tend to be averaged over time. In other words, early on in the placement process the support needs can be quite high and easily exceed the amount of funding available. When averaged with lower needs for other placements with greater tenure, it can work out well for all concerned. There is no simple magic formula for this, and funding sources need to allow for this kind of flexibility if quality support services are going to be financially feasible. Developing a trained, professional staff requires a reasonable level of consistent revenue. Dramatic fluctuations in funding lead to budgeting nightmares, high staff turnover, and quality problems.

It also follows that job-support services are not some kind of generic commodity that may be auctioned off to the lowest bidder. No one would attempt this with medical services, and the professionalism of the supports provided in our field is no different. Quality costs, but in the long term it is always the best value.

Myth 4: Anyone can do this work

As discussed earlier, some funding agencies have adopted this myth as a way to reduce expenses. They seem to think that dragging a client around and helping them fill out job applications is all that is necessary. Once they are hired (which will sometimes happen) the client is turned loose. This approach is similar to the parable about spreading seeds in the hope that one will take root somewhere. Unfortunately, this does not work and causes great damage in the process. Employers who are burned refuse to consider additional hiring. Clients who are traumatized refuse to try another job. The money spent in this way is usually wasted and ends up costing far more in the long run when clients are placed again and again into ill-matched jobs.

Myth 5: Home issues are not work issues and should never be addressed by employment staff

We utilize a comprehensive approach that has many similarities to progressive corporate management. Supplemental programs, such as employee counseling services for financial, emotional, or other problems, are not universal but they do exist. They recognize the fact that keeping good employees sometimes requires offering some extra help. Everyone runs into serious problems at times, and only the most ruthless employers fail to recognize that fact.

Our clients will tend to have even more problems because of the nature of their disabilities. They are almost all in the lower income bracket. A great many have medical issues. Their social opportunities are more limited (which means they are often more lonely). They have a much harder time establishing themselves in their communities and receiving recognition. There are many other "non-work" issues.

It should be clear that these so-called non-work issues do, in fact, often end up affecting work at some point. Absenteeism, emotional problems, stress, loneliness, financial setbacks, and so on can all harm the performance of an employee to the point where it *does* become a work issue. Employers can and do address these with their employees at times. Our approach simply recognizes that fact and asserts that these ancillary problems do warrant some assistance on occasion. There is no substitute for common sense and good judgment in these matters, so there are always limitations and conditions. Nevertheless, excluding them from consideration is naïve at best.

Myth 6: Replicate the perfect model

The perfect model does not exist. There are too many variables, too many individual differences, too many economic differences, and too many other factors for this to be possible. In spite of all this, some models have been hyped as the "answer," or the "solution." In other cases an organization claims itself to be the "leader in its field." Local economies and labor markets alone are such huge variables that it is impossible to import a model from another area and expect the same results.

Back in the 1980s this author went on a number of wild goose chases in pursuit of the perfect model for employment. One organization claimed to have placed nearly all of its clients into community-based employment in less than 18 months. After a journey of a thousand miles and a much closer look, it was discovered that none of the clients "placed" earned any money. None. All of them were "volunteers." This is just another way of saying they had no value to their employers. (Volunteering in and of itself can be a wonderful thing, but it should not be used as a charade for real employment.) The organization defended this by stating that placement came first in their model, and they hoped that employers would someday begin paying for the clients' work. If the organization does not see value in their clients' work, it is folly to presume employers will.

In another case claims were wildly exaggerated and the jobs in the community were actually goals rather than achievements. In still another case, an enclave of workers in a prominent high-tech industry was cited by government agencies as being "the model" to be emulated and replicated throughout the industry. A visit and subsequent scrutiny of the budget turned up a cost per person that was roughly 400 percent of the funds normally possible for these kinds of support services. They rationalized it by stating that they were simply showing this kind of model was possible, and not that it was financially feasible. That little detail was left for others to figure out. This enclave came to a screeching halt when the massive subsidies ended. A model that is not financially feasible and sustainable is not, in fact, a model worth considering.

Our entire argument for employment is based on a handful of principles rather than a specific model. Principles apply universally, and in all locations. Models do not. They do, however, contribute to mythology.

15

*H*ealth, Diet, Exercise, and Socialization

Our focus thus far has concentrated primarily on employment. We now turn our attention to some of those "non-work" concerns we discussed briefly in the previous chapter. These can ultimately affect our clients' abilities to become or remain employed. An organization or entity hired to provide employment supports may believe these issues to be wholly out of their range of concern. However, each is truly important for all members of an individual's support team to understand and consider during the planning process as well as thereafter.

Health

It is generally accepted that persons with developmental disabilities tend to have more medical issues than non-disabled people. This is just part of the equation we need to accept. What we should not accept is an attitude that there is nothing we can do to assist in minimizing the problems that our clients must face.

Health issues can and do create job losses. Sometimes it is from unacceptable attendance or inability to perform a physical function or a side-effect of a medication. Whatever the reason, all members of the support team need to work cooperatively in both prevention activities and accessing appropriate treatment.

Prevention of problems is the natural starting place. Providing commonsense counseling on basic matters such as hand-washing, hygiene, and other simple measures is something that anyone can do. Some of our clients have wonderful family support where extraordinary care and counsel is a given. Some live in poverty where these basics may be neglected. Others live in residential programs with inconsistent attention to preventative measures. Still others live independently and do not have identified supports for health matters.

Once a problem is actually diagnosed, the quality of medical care provided varies in a similar fashion. Healthcare professionals do not always provide the same level of service to our clients as they would to more affluent and effective self-advocates. In these situations team members need to step up and assertively demand quality care. This is the kind of activity that does not routinely appear on a job description dedicated solely to employment matters. Our job description, however, permits it discreetly in the section which states "provide counseling on matters which interfere with their ability to remain gainfully employed." Discretion and professional judgment are always required, but we should not run away when there is no other option available for our clients. An excellent strategy is to have a medical person, such as a registered nurse, as a consultant to offer advice to staff in difficult situations. Experience has demonstrated that this can help in the advocacy for proper medical attention.

Here is a classic example of this kind of problem. Many years ago a client was having severe reactions to a seizure-control medication. The family was not particularly adept at dealing with doctors and kept repeating that the family physician did not see a problem. With their permission, we reviewed the client's medical history with a consultant. We discovered that the epilepsy diagnosis had been made by a general practitioner (rather than a neurologist) many years earlier after report of a single alleged seizure. Our client had been taking an older, outdated seizure medication for years as a result. We persuaded the family to seek a second opinion from a reputable neurologist. The neurologist determined that the diagnosis was erroneous and no medication was required at all. The point is that we are not trying to play doctor in situations like these. Rather, we employ a fundamental principle regarding healthcare services: *If the client were our own family member, what would we want to happen and how would we advocate for it?* Using this principle, and explaining it to those in charge of securing healthcare for our client, we are often able to facilitate getting second opinions, a more appropriate kind of practitioner, or a review of potentially harmful prescriptions. The worst possible response is a shrug of the shoulders and a nonchalant "it's not our job." We cannot control these things, but we can certainly have a very positive influence when we are careful and use good judgment.

One problem that appears far too frequently is inadequate monitoring of medications. Many of our clients are poor self-reporters regarding symptoms. Sometimes the dosage is wrong but is left in place without a timely review of its efficacy. In some cases clients are seeing several doctors and receiving multiple prescriptions without the doctors being aware of this fact. Sometimes medications are not taken at all. Very serious problems can result from any of these situations. Employment specialists often see the effects of these problems but may not have any direct connection to the medical services being coordinated.

This is where good, professional advocacy is important. Even if the advocacy consists of making some telephone calls and asking questions about what is going on, it may help to ameliorate many of these problems. In more serious cases a written request for a review can be warranted. When this is done solely on the basis of the client's best interests, it can be very effective in getting results.

Diet

We live in an age where an unprecedented number of people in the general population are obese. Diabetes Type 2 is now considered to be a virtual epidemic. Our clients are not immune from this. They suffer through the same temptations of fattening fast food and prepared foods with low nutritional content. Poor diets can and do produce problems in work performance.

Sometimes these effects are not severe, but in other cases they may threaten employment. We have worked with a number of individuals who require regular blood sugar testing to maintain the equilibrium necessary for basic functioning. In these cases it is necessary to have full team support for a carefully planned and implemented diet. When this is neglected the individual can suffer weakness, fainting, and even emergency trips to the hospital. Home providers and other support team members need to embrace the need for a healthy diet to overcome these problems.

In other cases the effects may be rather gross and embarrassing. When an employer complained once about excessive time our client spent in the bathroom, we discovered there was a well-ingrained habit of purchasing as many as six large candy bars every day. The result was a bad case of repetitive diarrhea, which sometimes manifested itself while working. Unfortunately, traditional physicians often react to a problem of this nature by merely writing a prescription for something to treat the symptom while completely ignoring the cause. The real solution should be a change of diet so that healthier foods replace those causing the root problem. Borrowing a term from database management, "garbage in, garbage out." In most cases the simplest solution is the best.

Similar issues come up regarding constipation, lack of energy, excessive medical appointments, and even on-the-job accidents. Many are preventable with healthier diets. Successful interventions are possible but difficult. It must be understood that habits like fast food can be similar to addictions to drugs. Habits are hard to break, but simply giving up is the worst option. Sometimes well-meaning members of a support team will spout a platitude like "It's his choice, so let him do it." This sounds reasonable at first, but it does not stand the test of truly informed consent. The client is almost never absolutely clear about the long-term damage that may come from an unhealthy diet, and it should be the responsibility of the team to help them gain that reality of perspective.

The only truly effective method is a unified team effort to inform, persuade, nudge, and support the individual as they gradually make changes. A professional nutritionist, in a consulting capacity, can be a real asset in recommending healthier choices. Working directly with a primary care physician to prescribe alternatives may help immensely. Positive feedback from team members for progress can be very rewarding. Enrollment in weight-reduction programs is also a good idea and provides another reinforcement through socialization. The bottom line here is that problems seldom exist in isolation, and we must be willing to accept that fact and take positive, supportive action.

Exercise

Healthy exercise is the twin of healthy diet. We face the exact same kinds of problems here as people spend more and more time wasting away in front of televisions and less time exercising. The team approach used for diet applies equally well here also, but there are some advantages. First, the right job match may create a healthy level of exercise because it is needed to do the work. A customer service clerk at a market is a good example here. The position requires constant standing and walking, virtually ensuring that the employee gets exercise every day. Placing a client who is obese into a completely sedentary job is asking for trouble later on. A good job match would have a reasonable level of physical activity involved.

There are other helpful measures to address outside the workplace. Transportation may sometimes be arranged so that a modest walk to a bus stop becomes a daily routine. Sometimes people want to eliminate any effort for a client out of a desire to help. This is obviously an unwise choice. Reasonable amounts of exercise should be encouraged and praised in the same way as healthy diets. Participation in a team sport, Special Olympics, or at a local gym can also help.

Socialization

One of the many benefits of working in a community-based job is that there are opportunities to socialize with a broad array of people. Sometimes the opportunity alone leads to satisfying relationships with co-workers or others just like it does for the rest of us. This can be one of the best kinds of rewards because it just makes people feel connected and valued for whom they are. The act of assisting a client to become employed has ramifications extending well beyond the workplace itself. Most of these are positive, but we do need to be aware of some potential problems as well.

Not all new friends or relationships are automatically desirable ones. Workplaces can harbor some unsavory characters who may see our client as a potential target. Exploitation does occur and may be found in a variety of forms. One of these is financial, with our client being used for loans or rip-offs on property. It was very sad to learn some years ago that a client had sold an almost new, and very expensive, television for a few dollars to a scheming co-worker. Another variation on this happens when the client is persuaded to buy something at an inflated price. Our clients with trusted home providers and supportive families usually manage to steer clear of these problems, but those who are more independent can fall victim. Once again we confront the dilemma of wanting to encourage independence while still agonizing when we know someone is acting in a predatory fashion toward our client.

Solid team support and problem-solving is always important in finding solutions. However, sometimes an old-fashioned technique has also worked effectively. In these cases we simply came in and told the predator we were watching what was going on, and they backed off. The mere fact of knowing that clients have people looking out for them is an excellent deterrent when used judiciously.

We live in an age where illegal drug use is far too common. Some workplaces unwittingly serve to provide connections and potential customers. This kind of problem will also be more likely with the more independent clients we serve. One warning sign is when new "friends" with questionable motives begin to appear under suspicious circumstances. For example, once a client announced that a new "friend" had moved into his apartment almost overnight. This rather nasty character was looking for a free lunch, a place to stay, and a home base for selling drugs. A rapid intervention worked, but this is not possible if there is insufficient contact.

Our clients do succumb to drugs on occasion, although this does tend to be quite rare. When it happens it is a sad business but it needs to be confronted in a way similar to that used for other employees. If there is a policy requiring a treatment program it should be put into place along with any disciplinary actions normally used. In other words, our client should be treated as any other employee. Engaging in overprotectiveness or denial will only exacerbate the problems in the long run.

There are also sexual predators who view our clients as easy targets. The good news is that special education and advocacy programs teach awareness of this kind of abuse so many of our clients have been well prepared. Nevertheless, potentially disastrous situations do require steadfast alertness. Predators often make contacts through family connections, but workplaces can harbor these types as well. Persons with developmental disabilities become victims far more often than the general population.

Good team planning, supports, and ongoing communication are the most effective tools once again. The fact that risks exist is a very poor rationale for denying a person all the benefits that accrue from being fully involved as members of their communities. It is easy to be too sheltering with some of our clients, and yet we should always be cognizant of certain kinds of risk factors. The risk–benefit analysis we described earlier is the most effective way to sort out a good strategy. For example, if we are working on a placement plan for a young woman who is rather naïve about these matters we should build in safeguards against things like riding home from work with male co-workers. Males are also targets on occasion so we should be equally diligent with them.

We should view socialization as a fundamental human need and not as just a luxury. The fact is that our clients need to be connected with other people on a regular basis, and in ways that allow them to develop healthy relationships on a variety of levels. These include work relationships, friends, social activities, and romantic relationships. Assisting our clients to become and remain employed does not normally include plans for addressing these kinds of issues. Nevertheless, we still need to be aware of them and, to a certain limited extent, work to reduce artificial barriers that can arise. If we fail to do this, we should not be surprised when there are consequences.

In many cases it does not require sophisticated plans to do simple things with wonderful benefits. We might try to arrange a work schedule that allows our client to participate in a favorite Special Olympics activity. We could encourage (and perhaps even go along the first time) them to join a company bowling league. We could arrange an introduction to the pastor of a church which has a companion program. We could arrange an introduction with another client who may have very similar interests and needs. We could advocate for another service provider, such as a residential program, to develop more social activities. We could also suggest vacation trips or outings with organizations specializing in providing these to persons with disabilities.

There are many other kinds of opportunities we could explore and encourage when appropriate. This is done with the knowledge that a sad, lonely person can bring their unhappiness into the workplace. This does happen, and it will affect job performance. A story told too often is about a client who heads home from work, sits in front of the television all evening, and repeats this tedium all over again day after day. For very little effort we can sometimes create opportunities for a much more fulfilling life for our clients.

16

*O*rganizations,
Structures, and Ethics

This chapter is intended primarily for non-profit organizations, although many of the concepts mentioned might be helpful in other situations as well. Non-profit organizations serving people with disabilities often provide a variety of services. These may include direct employment, supported employment, activity or recreation programs, residential support services, transportation, and others. Our focus is obviously on supported individual employment, but this part of the organization's activities requires a comprehensive embrace if it is to be successful. The alternative is a "silo" approach where departments function independently without concern for the success of the organization as a whole. This scenario is not rare and is caused by a lack of effective leadership.

It has to begin with a commitment from the top level of management and governing board. There will have to be allocations of limited resources and this means some sacrifice in some areas while this new (or expanded) service is nurtured. Sometimes interdepartment rivalries spring up and it is up to the leadership to establish the long-term goals as organizational priorities. This is the part where bridge funding is necessary to dislodge the organization from the inertia holding it in its present place. All of the techniques covered in the discussion on financial success come into play here.

An important concept to instill is that greater financial success in the long term will be only be possible with intelligent investment in the short term.

The reality here is that not everyone may buy into the new goal. This can be a tough challenge for leadership but it must be addressed. If not, subtle sabotage may occur in a variety of forms. If, for example, candidates for individual placement jobs are to be referred from existing sheltered employment operations, these could suffer from the loss of some of their most productive workers. A focus on the mission of the organization and the benefits to the clients is the only real answer here. Resistance can happen, but it must be overcome within a reasonable period of time. If resistance continues it may be necessary to remove the problem person(s) from the organization.

One of the best ways to chart a new course with a new goal for the organization is through the use of a planning retreat. Getting away from the usual surroundings over a weekend is sometimes the only way to have the time to fully explore such a large undertaking. Including management with the governing board allows everyone to have input while ensuring that a goal has the best chance of being realized. It is not a purely democratic process in that the outcome does not necessarily come from a majority vote. Rather, it is an opportunity to discuss ideas in depth and develop a level of understanding and commitment that is otherwise unattainable. If the desired goal is a transition to a new or expanded individual jobs program, time must be spent researching how the goal can be achieved and what the benefits should be. A great way to do this is to bring in a guest from a similar organization already established in this endeavor. Any big change entails both gains and costs, and these may be explored in detail in this kind of environment. The bottom line must always be the best interests of the clients to be served, and with this in mind there really is no good argument against a successful jobs program.

It may be necessary to start with a new look at the mission statement of the organization. The mission should be broad enough to cover a wide variety of endeavors while centering on assisting clients to realize their full potential. It is a self-evident truth that the best and most independent jobs possible should be a goal with this type of mission.

Sometimes an argument is made that the best job is the one with the highest wages. This argument is made to defend sheltered employment jobs needed to fulfill profitable contracts. Some very profitable contracts do exist because of government subsidies and "set-asides." The pricing on these is determined by costs incurred plus profit. High wages can, therefore, be passed along as costs incurred. These contracts are not bid for competitively and can greatly exceed a market-based price. Organizations sometimes succumb to the temptation of these profits at the expense of following their mission. Scandals have occurred when executive pay has subsequently skyrocketed, sometimes into the millions.

The argument based strictly on higher wages is wrong because its premise is wrong. A sheltered job denies opportunities to clients to become part of the greater society in an integrated setting with all its benefits (and, yes, risks). There are far too many examples of an organization securing a well-paying contract and then steering clients into the jobs created. This serves the organization and its staff at the expense of the clients because they lose the right to choose for themselves. Artificially high wages end up creating *dependence* on the organization rather than *independence* achieved by real productivity. Higher wages are necessary for financial empowerment, but they should be paid because the person has become productive and valuable to a willing employer. They should not come as a result of contractual manipulation based on dependence.

Any system providing services to people deals with a very limited amount of resources. As a result, there are almost always more individuals with developmental (and other severe) disabilities than there are jobs readily available. Waitlists for these employment services are not uncommon, as well as backlogs of people still working in sheltered environments. This means that resources must be expended wisely and always within the mission of the organization. When a lucrative contract is landed, it is not unusual to see the organization "recruiting" persons with disabilities to supply the workforce. This recruiting effort is invariably evidence that the priorities are upside down. An easy way to detect this is to note that the recruiting efforts often say things like "preference given to persons with disabilities," or "persons with disabilities are encouraged to apply." What this word trickery really means is that the contract becomes the priority and people will be hired to get it done regardless of whether they are truly disabled or not.

A far better way to employ persons with disabilities is with the "affirmative business" model. This is an honest model that does not employ deceptions such as portraying non-disabled workers as disabled simply to exaggerate statistics needed for a government contract. These kinds of deceptions are sometimes exposed. In one, the primary "disability" group served was discovered to be people for whom English was a second language, a far cry from the intent and letter of the law authorizing these contracts. Unscrupulous executives sometimes ply the sympathy for disabled persons while lining their own pockets. Vaguely worded recruiting efforts are one signal that the organization has allowed its mission to be distorted.

There is another concept affecting these kinds of situations. It is known as "creaming," and it refers to the act of securing funds to serve people with more severe needs but, instead, weeding them out and replacing them with people with minor disabilities or none whatsoever. This is done because it is more profitable. This author cringed some years ago when he heard an executive at a very large non-profit organization announce he was gradually ending services to persons with developmental disabilities. The reason given was that there was "just not enough money in it" and they were not able to fulfill the organization's huge government contracts. It takes far less resources (i.e. money) to employ people whose needs are minimal. When a contract is secured the temptation to "cream" is often too much for some executives to ignore. This creates a clear conflict of interest in that executive pay is usually a function of the size of the budget. Bigger budgets create bigger executive salaries, but they do not necessarily result in better, more integrated jobs for our clients. The decisions of executives may be compromised when their compensation is determined under the dark cloud of "creaming." As Upton Sinclair once stated, "It is difficult to get a man to understand something when his salary depends upon his not understanding it." Governing boards need to look at large contracts from this perspective, and should seriously question how the contracts will promote integration and independence before approving them. *The principle is that those with the most severe disabilities should be served first because they have the most severe challenges to overcome.*

The common denominator to be found in virtually all of the examples related to mission drift is a conflict of interests. In other words, decision-makers are in situations where their objectivity is compromised by the temptation of personal or organizational gain at the expense of clients or others. In recent years we have seen countless examples of disastrous financial results in industry after industry, ranging from banking to real-estate to manufacturing, and many others. When the dynamics of these disasters are revealed we almost invariably find an unattended conflict of interest at the root. One of the most common scenarios is that of a CEO who has the power to steer money to himself by compromising the integrity of his business operation. Our field is not immune from this kind of profiteering. It is a lesson that all governing boards should apply as they determine policy.

We have come a long, long way from the days when persons with developmental disabilities were either institutionalized or warehoused in segregated facilities out of sight of the rest of the world. In some areas we have made tremendous strides. In others we still have a long road in front of us. Our evolution as a society will be judged in part by our willingness and ability to bring our most vulnerable citizens into the world as equals rather than burdens. This challenge is a critical component in the struggle for equality and civil rights for everyone.

We can meet this challenge.

*A*ppendix

Principles of Job Success

- Persons with developmental disabilities want to be seen as people who have a legitimate role in society and in the workforce. They do not want to be seen as merely "disabled" or "handicapped." They want the same things as the rest of us.

- We should assist our clients in realizing their individual potential, whatever that might be.

- Job success means that the client likes the job, the employer likes having the client as an employee, and the job continues for at least six months.

- Most job losses are caused by problems in the social, rather than technical, arena of workplaces.

- All stakeholders have a perspective, but no single perspective is sufficient alone.

- A major change like a new job first requires trust, and the trust must be earned.

- The client and key stakeholders must also establish ownership in helping to achieve the job goal.

- Individual job placements, nurtured and allowed to gradually mature with natural supports, are the best overall model of employment.

- Employers tend to underrepresent minor issues but these will grow over time into major ones.

- Deal with all issues, even minor ones, within one business day.

- More time and effort will be spent on dealing with social interactions and their potential difficulties than on all other issues combined.

- If the client were our own family member, what would we want to happen and how would we advocate for it?

- Clients with the most severe disabilities should be served first because they have the most severe challenges to overcome.

*I*ndex

information gathering
about employer 78
informed consent 64–6
integration 69
intellectual impairments
13
intermediaries 67
interviews 34, 36–7,
47
introductions 144

"job carving" 56–7
job coaching 93
attendance 94
co-worker
relationships
103
expectations 94
feedback 95–7
issues 102
natural supports 101
problems 97
solving 98–9
support 99, 133
purpose of 93–4
role of supervisor 94
job creation 20
see also small
business
community
job description 44
essential functions
of 76
placement plan 50
job development
corporate 53, 67
individual 53, 67
job development plan
41
challenges 44
team signatures 48,
52
template 41–2

job development
strategy 46
"objectives" 46
placement plan 51
responsibilities 47
job goal 45–6
job matching 59
placement plan 51
job longevity 23
job loss 128
job matching 58–9, 79
job placement programs
18
job placement staff 29
job success 13, 27, 79,
101, 128
job value 12

key staff 67

labels 11, 12
unintentional 12
learning new skills 23
legal loopholes 72
light bulb moment
38–9, 75

mainstream employment
20
management
models 113
theories 29
marketing 54
medical information 33,
138–9
medications 139
minimal qualifications
20
mission drift 149
myths 131–6

natural supports 71–3

evolution of 101
myths 71
nurture of 73
responsibility 71
negligence 64
see also disclosure
networking 46–7
non-disabled 12, 28
non-disabled workers
productivity 23
respect 69
non-profit organizations
13, 107
mission 17
volunteers 19
"norm" 63

ongoing support 74
on-the-job training 81
see also training
opportunities 12
overheads 112
overprotectiveness 66,
101

"paraplegic" see labels
payroll 61
perceived deficiency 12
perception 12–13
perfect model, the 135
personal hygiene 102,
138
persons with
developmental
disabilities 20
advantages to
employers 24
as pioneer 69
behavior of family
members 28
dangers to 143
dignity 30

supervision 76
"supported
 employment" 14,
 24
support team 64, 99,
 133
systems and
 organizations 13

"Tarzan Principle, The"
 104
 see also career
 development
task analysis 79
team support 59, 99,
 142
technical competence
 36
technical requirements
 76
"three degrees of
 separation" 53–4
trade associations 68
training 81
 aids 123
 checklist 124, 125
 correct procedures
 86
 debriefing 124
 demonstration 84
 ergonomics 85
 job analysis 81–2,
 84
 motion 86
 new employees 84
 observation 87
 prevention of fatigue
 85
 psychological
 concepts 86
 quality assurance
 85–6

quality control 84,
 87–8
 sampling 87–8
 reasons for 88
 tools 89
 adaptive
 equipment
 90–1
 media and
 graphics 89
 visual schedules
 89–90
transportation 45
 placement plan 51
trust 35, 97
turnover cost 22
turnover expenses
 savings in 23

understanding 19
 informed consent
 64–6
 in job carving 56
 the client 31, 75
 the employer 55
 the job 75–80,
 82–3
unionized workforce 70
"unrealistic
 expectations" 37
upper management 67
US Department of
 Labor 63
 see also sub-minimum
 wages

visiting employers 47
volunteers 19, 135

wage levels 26, 42
 placement plan 49
 see also rate of pay

waiting lists 147
wheelchair
 working from a 90
work-activity programs
 109
work crews 110
"work experience" 44
work performance 22
work schedule 76
 changes to 76